the Quintessential Searcher

The Wit & Wisdom of Barbara Quint

Edited by
Marylaine Block

Information Today, Inc.

Medford, New Jersey

First printing, August 2001

The Quintessential Searcher:
The Wit and Wisdom of Barbara Quint

Copyright © 2001 by Information Today, Inc.

A CIP catalog record for this book is available from the Library of Congress

ISBN 1-57387-114-1

Publisher: Thomas H. Hogan, Sr.
Editor-in-Chief: John B. Bryans
Managing Editor: Deborah R. Poulson
Production Manager: M. Heide Dengler
Copy Editor: Susan Muaddi Darraj
Designers: Jacqueline Walter and Kara Mia Jalkowski

For a publications catalog, contact the publisher at 609-654-6266
or 800-300-9868 (EST), or log onto www.infotoday.com

Printed in Canada

TABLE OF CONTENTS

Chapter 1
THE ART OF SEARCHING 17

Chapter 2
ON LIBRARIANS 29

Chapter 3

THE INTERNET 77

Chapter 4

DATABASE VENDORS 85

Chapter 5

SCHOLARLY PUBLISHING 133

Chapter 6

RANDOM MUSINGS 147

Chapter 7
WORDS TO LIVE BY 175

Chapter 8
BQ ON BQ 179

Chapter 9
BQ'S FANS SPEAK OUT 197

A NOTE ON SELECTION AND ARRANGEMENT

The easy part of editing the book was reading through Barbara's works and selecting the paragraphs and pages that made me say, "Wow."

As I selected and copied quotes, they started falling into obviously logical chapters for each of her main concerns and audiences: librarians, the Internet, vendors and databases, advice on searching, etc. Within the broad subjects, obvious sub-themes appeared—for database vendors, for example, dissatisfaction with products and pricing, alarm at their failure to respond to the Net, and suggestions on what they could do to survive.

Originally, I organized the quotes in each chapter in chronological order, so that we could see how Barbara's ideas evolved over time, but there was no flow to it when I did it that way. The purely chronological construction was jumpy and illogical, interrupted by events, large and small. I found myself having to write too much commentary explaining the quotes, which I didn't like, since the book is about Barbara, not me. Instead, I rearranged the quotes to develop a logical flow of ideas and themes, so that each quote informed the next, regardless of when it was written. I didn't want to interrupt the flow with full Chicago-style citations, but I have supplied enough documentation for each quote so that readers can find the entire article and see how Barbara developed any given idea.

On several occasions, Barbara has summarized her ideas about various topics in the form of "Quint's Laws." I have used these throughout as a kind of punctuation.

At the suggestion of my editors at Information Today, Inc., I have added brief introductions to each chapter to explain the context and background for Barbara's musings. I have also inserted occasional explanations and substitutions in brackets and italics.

ACKNOWLEDGMENTS

I would like to thank the people without whom this book would not have been possible, starting with Barbara Quint, who has spent the past 15 years writing words that fully warrant the title "Wit and Wisdom." She has offered me both bibliography and encouragement in the project. My thanks also to John B. Bryans, Editor-in-Chief of books at Information Today, for his leap of faith in believing I could pull this project off, for his editorial support, and for the book's title. And finally, my eternal gratitude to the full-text databases which provided many of the articles I used, and to the inventors of the greatest technological achievement of the 20th century, "copy and paste."

INTRODUCTION

This book is the result of the happiest of accidents. When I sent Information Today's John Bryans a copy of a review I'd done of one of his books, he offered me two more books to review. I passed on those, and said I'd be sure to let him know when I really wanted to get my hands on a new book from Information Today, for instance, hint, hint, *The Wit and Wisdom of Barbara Quint*. He wrote back and told me he'd wanted to publish such a collection for a long time, but hadn't been able to find an editor for the project. Would I, by chance, be interested?

Though I have never done anything remotely like this before, of course I said yes—what an opportunity! I've admired Barbara ("bq," as she's known to her readers) from the moment I first encountered one of her columns in *Searcher*. Each time I read a new one, my admiration grows —and as her editor, I've read everything she's written since 1986, including her monthly columns in *Wilson Library Bulletin* from 1986-1995, in *Database Searcher* from 1985-1992, in *Information Today* from 1992 to the present, in her own *Searcher* from 1993 to the present, and in miscellaneous articles and addresses published elsewhere.

Who is Barbara? The quintessential searcher (and I'd say that even if it weren't a good pun). Don't just take my word for it. In an article in the September 1991 *Information Today*,

Nancy Melin Johnson said: "She's simply a fantastically knowledgeable and dedicated online expert … I can't think of one single online searcher who wouldn't bet the company on her." Mick O'Leary is even more rhapsodic in the May-June 1993 issue of *Link-Up*:

> What Clapton is to the guitar, what Jordan is to the court, Barbara Quint is to online search-ing—the pro the other pros admire. She is well known as a researcher, consultant, author, speaker, and editor. Whichever hat she is wear-ing, she is always the Ralph Nader of the online world, an articulate and relentless advocate for the online consumer. (The Nader comparison is not perfect; Ralph is quite proper and a little grim, but Barbara's take-no-prisoners style and whiplash sense of humor guarantee standing-room-only crowds wherever she speaks.)

This is a woman with an incisive intelligence that cuts straight to the heart of any issue. She has one of the world's most finely honed crap detectors. Furthermore, she says exactly what she believes, no matter how sacred the ox she's goring, with a deadly wit that's nonetheless so good-humored her victims might not even notice right away that they're bleeding.

She took on the database vendors on whom our profession depends, bawling them out for offering us inferior products with inadequate documentation and expecting us to pay dia-mond prices for shabby zircons. (After one lengthy and costly search that yielded a few scrubby citations, she snorted, "$84.14 is *answer* money, not citation money.")

She took vendors to task for being years late and several dollars short in noticing that the Internet was offering better service than they were, free of charge.

She took on the scholarly publishing industry, the folks who get their research for free from scholars, and then sell the research back to the universities and government agencies who sponsored it at mind-boggling subscription rates that wipe out library budgets.

Years ago—before libraries banded together for massive digitizing projects like JSTOR, before the government came up with its BioMed Web publishing initiative, before the courts virtually put Westlaw out of business by publishing their decisions directly on the Net—Barbara proposed that government and university researchers should publish their own scholarship directly and cut out the middlemen.

Barbara has even taken on her own profession. She understood that databases and the Internet were going to force librarians to start all over again and learn an entirely new way of doing things. She even sympathized with them. But she also realized, well before the rest of us, that the Net was our competition, that its search engines might answer people's questions well enough to make them feel they didn't have to go to a library ever again.

So she said, hey, things are tough all over. Get used to it. If the Net can do some things we've always done just as well, let it. Use what's already been done there and get on with the tasks that *only* information professionals can do.

She reminded librarians that our calling is to serve our patrons. What were we planning to do, she asks—deprive them of database searching because it's too expensive? Deprive them of the Internet, the world's biggest reference collection, because we don't know how to use it? Let our hapless end-users flounder because they don't know how to search it?

Nonsense, said Barbara. Our responsibility to end-users "should be to ensure that no one gets hurt, or at least not fatally."

In fact, she told us, the Net is a rare opportunity to offer expanded services, to do things we've never even been able to dream about: serve our clients 24/7/365, provide reference to distance users by e-mail or real-time chat, offer database searching and immediate download of full-text articles, and more.

Barbara has a habit of seeing the future years before it gets around to happening. In 1986, she told librarians who claimed not to have enough money for database service that, instead of spending money building branch libraries, they should invest in databases, wire every home in the city so that users could search library catalogs and databases electronically, and maybe even equip a fleet of motor scooters with baskets and send them around town delivering books and other library materials to our users' doors.

In 1993, she talked about reading a "customized morning newspaper displayed on our electronic mail service or rolling off our fax machine." OK, she didn't exactly foresee the World Wide Web, but she sure visualized the things people would do with it when it became available. Maybe Barbara was a little aggrieved that nobody believed her. In 1997, she wrote:

> I told you, World, that Online was the way to go. I told you, Information Industry, that someday this stuff would reach the masses. I told you, Techies, that someday people would buy computers just to

make their modems work. I told you, Librarians,
that people would expect information to pour out
of a computer like water from a tap."

But though Barbara is swift to point out where we have fallen short, she is equally swift to congratulate us on what we do right. She believes librarians will survive because, with our trained genius for finding, evaluating, and organizing information, we are the logical ones to tame the anything-goes world of the Net. We are also the only people with an ethical obligation to protect users from "the dangers of inaccurate, overpriced, dangerous data, from the perils of relying on the unreliable, and sinking into virtually baseless virtual realities."

Barbara taught librarians the necessity of complaining to vendors in order to get them to improve the product. But she also told them to compliment and promote vendors who create good products and pay attention to customer suggestions.

Vendors appreciate her as a tough but fair reviewer of new databases and technologies, and an endorsement from her is welcomed as both a proud accomplishment and a selling point.

After all, she wants vendors to survive—her pained tone with them is the one we might use to dissuade a dear friend bent on suicide. She has offered them detailed suggestions on how to improve their products and services. If they weren't visionaries enough to see the possibilities of the newly wired world, she could do it for them. She showed them how they could turn the ephemeral nature of the "cheap but flighty" Internet to their advantage.

She pointed out that vendors could archive newsgroups, newspaper and magazine articles, and documents that would otherwise get dumped from their Web sites to make room for the new. She told them they could provide added value in their full-text article databases by contracting with authors for continuing updates of articles, and by hot-linking Web-based bibliographic citations so that people could follow them up effortlessly.

Mind you, I don't always agree with Barbara. Because of her corporate background, she believes that information delivery dwarfs all other library functions. Having spent my life in public and college libraries, I am equally convinced that library users care just as passionately about the library's collection, its building, and its public and private spaces as they do about its information service.

But that's a minor disagreement. I've spent the past several months virtually inside Barbara's head, and I have enjoyed every minute of it. She is funny, acerbic, and insightful. If she has a deservedly healthy ego, she also has the grace to laugh at herself. Musing about what measuring stick she could use to assess her career, she briefly considered her writing and her editing before she hit on the best answer: "Let's count my career accomplishments in terms of gripes. With this column I celebrate my 10,000th complaint and hereby award a Virtual Medal to the Virtuous Me, the Loyal Order of the Eternal Nag."

I think you're going to enjoy getting to know bq as much as I have. At the very least, you'll understand why those of us who regard "tough broad" as the ultimate accolade view her as a goddess.

AN INTERVIEW WITH
BARBARA QUINT

Marylaine Block: How did you get from California school-girl, copying essays in their entirety out of encyclopedias, to librarian? What went into the choice, other than the realization that, "Oops, now I have to make a living, what does a degree in the humanities qualify me to do?"

Barbara Quint: In large part, the decision to become a librarian was a by-product of my life's only financial coup. When I left high school, a local Catholic society gave me a one-semester scholarship to Immaculate Heart College, a liberal arts women's college in L.A. Turns out that IHC had a policy that, as long as you maintained a B+ or above grade point average, they would extend any scholarship. (Needless to say, the college is now defunct—fiscal realities being what they are. In fact, my high school has become a housing development. At this point, I probably couldn't provide documentary evidence of any education beyond the eighth grade.) Anyway, at the end of my undergraduate period, having looted the college treasury for three and a half years, I had the unbridled gall to ask them to pay for a year of graduate school, and the only graduate school they offered was for library science. Just another lucky break.

MB: Describe your work as a librarian, back in the days when Chemical Abstracts and Physics Abstracts were still in paper copy. What did you learn from it?

BQ: Mainly I learned how to suppress acro- and claustrophobia. In the Rand Corporation's library at that time, the copies of those ancient tools resided in the sub-basement. (The main library resided in the main basement. We had to chin ourselves to see light.) To reach the high stacks in low places where *Chem Abs* and *Sci Abs* resided, you had to go downstairs to this airless, dimly lit grotto and then clamber up and down rolling stairs to reach whatever volumes you needed. Needless to say, when online arrived—even in the guise of Texas Instruments TI700 barely luggable with its "wanna-wrestle?" acoustic coupler—I never saw that sub-basement again.

Initially, I hired on at Rand as a cataloger, but management used to assign us to the reference desk half a day a week, just to give the poor lone reference librarian time to breathe, I guess. I enjoyed it, particularly because I got a chance to chat with researchers. One day, I chatted away for 45 minutes (all right, an hour) with a researcher, while, unbeknownst to me, my boss, the head cataloger, cruised the area intermittently. She transferred to head of public services a few months later and drafted me to head up Reference, telling me that she figured I had the stuff it took after observing that conversation. Her actual language, as I recall, was, "Looks like you're not a phony or at least he couldn't figure it out." Life's second lesson: Doing the things you shouldn't do can sometimes do as much good as doing the things you should, especially if they feel right at the time.

MB: When did database searching come into your life, and how did you respond to it? As a non-techie, how did you deal with ever-changing hardware and software?

BQ: As head of Reference at the Rand Corporation, I had one assistant and, hardware-phobic as I was then (and still am to a great extent), I used my authority to assign online to her, not me. She was not very tall (except in spirit, in case she's reading this, and even if she's not). Suffice it to say, whenever she had to do a search, she had to trot up to the Computer Department and borrow a TI700, which came up above her waist, and drag it back through corridors stretching half the length of the building. Due to this abuse of power, I actually missed learning Rand's first online service, the AIMS-TWX, pre-Medline system.

Once we got a permanent machine, lazybones decided to get with the program. I started with SDC's ORBIT, then Dialog, then The New York Times Information Service, then LexisNexis, then CSC, then DTIC, then …. Suffice it to say, at one time our library accessed 31 commercial search services, each one with its own search protocols, more than any other library in the country at the time, I believe. For the ones we used rarely, we invented a standard protocol—call the customer support desk before every search. One of them got so tired of hearing from us that they just created downloadable files of search strategies and told us how to plug-and-play.

MB: Talk about SCOUG [*Southern California Online Users' Group*] if you would—how it started, what it does, how it's grown and changed over the years, and what you've gotten from it.

BQ: Remember I told you about that boss who shanghaied me into reference work? Well, one day back in the mid-1970s, I wandered into her office to complain about Dialog never offering training sessions in Southern California. "Honestly, here we are the second largest city in the country and they still make us all motor to Palo Alto like we were Peoria …." Finally, she got bored with my kvetching and told me to stop complaining and do something about it. Start an online users group and get them to come to us.

So I did. Our first meeting in 1976 was supremely auspicious. We invited the head of a "newbie" called Information Access Company (now part of Gale Group), which promised an online (and microfiche) alternative to H. W. Wilson's *Readers' Guide* called *Magazine Index*. Dick Kollin was that wonderful speaker and became a permanent and steady SCOUG-er through all the years since. After a wonderful initial address, he got hammered by a couple of UCLA reference librarians over a data quality issue. He gulped once and then promised to fix the problem, and, when we checked, turns out he did. There, in one session, was set the pattern for the ages—vendors teaching searchers, searchers teaching vendors, everyone teaching everyone else, and somewhere around, the hammer of consumer advocacy.

Ten years into SCOUG, still operating as we do today with no dues for membership and regular quality programs designed by users for users, all depending on the talent, vigor, generosity, and professional collegiality of volunteer leadership, we decided to launch an experimental retreat. Some of us fantasized that it would become an Aspen-like affair with vendor executives mixing with "real people" searchers as the years went by. Guess what? It did. Of course, the fact that the second retreat happened to coincide with the first major sale of Dialog and gave us a hot vendor topic that got national press coverage didn't hurt either.

MB: You must have already been well known in the searching community to be invited to write columns for *Wilson Library Bulletin* and *Information Today.* How did that come about? That is, how were you rousing rabble *before* you had a regular column?

BQ: Once again, luck—and readiness—is everything. One evening, I was all set to mail out a SCOUG flyer for an upcoming meeting. By sheer happenstance, I had happened to pick up three juicy pieces of online industry gossip, and I just couldn't resist sharing it. Since the flyer had an empty page just sitting there waiting, I wrote up the gossip and titled it "SCOUG Miscellany." Within a year, I was grinding out six or more single-spaced pages every two months filled with news, tips, problems, etc. (If now were then, it would have been a Webzine.) Sometimes the writing took me deep into the night, but, lucky me, Rand was open 24/7 even then (sigh). Online, Inc. got a hold of some copies and drew me into their conferences and even a little writing.

Then, one day in 1985, I got a call from Alan Meckler inviting me to edit and write a magazine called *Database Searcher.* I never looked back. A month or two before the new magazine was scheduled to start, I joined Meckler at a dinner he gave during the Online conference. Gingerly, I passed him a copy of the latest SCOUG Miscellany. Turns out he had hired me not only sight unseen, but sight unread. He read one page of my prose and spoke the words I want hacked into my tombstone: "I get it: Breezy but Profound."

MB: You've talked at length about how both librarians and database vendors need to adapt to the new give-it-away-free business model of the Internet. What signs have you seen that they are following your advice?

BQ: Clearly Factiva, specifically their Dow Jones Interactive side, has seen the light for some time. They have set a standard that searching shouldn't cost, only finding counts. Of course, Netters don't even like to pay then, so Dowjones.com now gives away a lot of useful data, while still offering to sell more. Of course, the publishers have the advantage over the database aggregator or search service since they own the product—or at least they did until the Tasini case came down.

In reality, no one has now or ever will offer "free" information. Someone always has to pay, since information costs to produce and distribute. The question is never whether someone will pay, but who. Some traditionals have begun to experiment with the Internet's dominant business model—advertiser/sponsor funding—usually in joint ventures with Net Newbies. We'll see how that works out, especially if or when the traditionals and their new partners find themselves going after the same dollar as their publisher suppliers. No matter what you hear, I believe advertising money for the Net will only grow. Since prime-time television's dominance over the nation's eyeballs collapsed under competition from cable, video, and now the Internet, advertisers need all the help they can get to put their messages in front of those eyeballs, wherever they are.

MB: Of all the things you do—edit, write, speak, organize conferences, think about where our technology is taking us—what have you enjoyed most?

BQ: Writing and speaking. I can still remember groaning when my contact at Mecklermedia called after receiving the first issue of *Database Searcher* from me and said I had to add an editorial. Now, writing my "Searcher's Voice" editorials, followed by that month's "Quint's Online" column for *Information Today*, marks the most enjoyable tasks of the month.

Speaking was great, though I do very little anymore. I loved to see all those shining faces and meet my readers, but two incidents on one of my last trips led me to the decision to get off the road. Dragging my bewheeled luggage through LAX at midnight on my way to Chicago, a guard greeted me with the spine-chilling words, "Oh, I know you. You're a regular, aren't you?" Then, on my way back from Chicago, a stewardess dragging her own bewheeled luggage looked around and said, "Oh, hi! Guess we're going to have you on our flight again. Nice to see you." Man! When they recognize you 2,500 miles from home in O'Hare airport, you have been on the road too long!

MB: Of all the things you learned in college and in library school, what has had the most long-term benefit for you?

BQ: A sense of history and a commitment to the information professional's service ethic. History isn't just what makes the papers. History happens to each one of us, to each family, to each company, to each community, to each nation. When you look at the world around you in different font sizes, so to speak, you learn a lot from the changing perspectives. For one thing, you learn how to shape your actions to try to help things go the way they should. Maybe it works, maybe it doesn't. But like G. K. Chesterton said in my favorite quote of all time, "A thing worth doing is worth doing badly."

As for commitment, I glimpsed a vision in library school that shaped my life. We information professionals, we librarians, if you will, serve the minds of humanity. We find the information people need to prolong their lives, protect their liberties, and ensure their pursuit of happiness. Put us on the trail and we will pursue answers over the face of the earth and beyond, until the resources or the interest dies out. With us, the only bad question is an unasked question. And we regard clients and their needs as heavenly charges— at least on the good days, we do.

MB: If you were asked to design a library school curriculum, what are the key things you think librarians and information professionals need to be able to do? What are the attributes of the ideal information professional, and have those changed over time?

BQ: Commitment. Belief in the service ethic, in our role as protectors and providers for the minds in our charge. The ideal information professional remains largely the same, just the tools have changed. But we must never get trapped by formats. We define our resources, they don't define us. The greatest gift the new technologies have provided is the chance to make permanent solutions to problems. In the past, we have had to do the same things over and over. As intermediaries, we got the same types of requests from the same types of users over and over. Now, when a question keeps coming up, we can record a permanent answer, or a permanent route to an answer, and mark that question forever completed.

At least we can if the sources we tap remain stable. The greatest task facing information professionals today is building flexible access to stable archives of digital information. We must build The Virtual Library that can provide all people with all answers all the time. Library school curricula must recognize that task and build the professional skill base to accomplish it. In a sense, this task only expands the commitment. In the past, no librarian could be expected to serve any but the minds in their constituency—their clients, their citizenry. They could only dream of fulfilling a commitment to all minds everywhere. Now technology has made that dream a possibility. It's our job to make it a reality.

MB: Who are your heroes in the information profession?

BQ: Oh no, you don't. Not in this life. Their names are written on my heart. Ask the coroner if you have to know. Hey! I have to live in this Third Millennium, you know.

MB: What do you do for fun (besides *Antiques Road Show*)?

BQ: Movies—just got digital cable, and my television-viewing opportunities have ballooned out of sight. Crossword puzzles—I still think measuring the skill and will to do crossword puzzles could define the potential of a candidate cataloger or indexer. Books from Amazon.com—"If you can read this message, please send help." E-commerce shopping—"Never mind. Too late."

MB: Are there any other unexpected sidelights on you that you'd like to share? A childhood longing to grow up to be Batman? A passion for collecting Barbie dolls?

BQ: Barbie Dolls!! Harumph. The other activity which has meant the most to me in my life is feminism. We started a Women's Lobby at my former employer that led to real change and real improvement. I even testified once in front of a visiting Congressional committee, though the members seemed rather sleepy at the time. I would be hard put to identify which tasks appealed more—working over vendors or working to free half the human race.

Actually, I guess benevolence with conflict was my destiny from childhood. My mother worked, and so I spent a lot of time after school watching television reruns of old movies, before the Homework Hammer arrived. My two favorite movie stars of all time were John Wayne and Barbara Stanwyck—feisty, fun, and a strong sense of integrity. Those were my childhood idols. Still are, come to think of it.

Chapter 1

THE ART OF SEARCHING

This is the standard Barbara Quint has set for searchers: their job is to translate the stated and unstated needs of the patron into the language of an information system they understand to its core. Like petroleum engineers who've mapped the geological strata, they know where to start drilling and which tools to use. They understand that the answers depend entirely on how well they ask the question. Like detectives, searchers let each new piece of information speak to them, suggesting additional questions to ask, other databases to search, new experts or organizations to consult. Searchers must then test their answers for authority and truth, and for the smile on the face of the patron.

Finding Out What the Patron Wants

"Tell me a story" is a good approach. Really get interested in what they're saying. Don't be thinking about it as a search topic. Think about the role it's going to play. Get them talking in their own terms, as though they are talking to a colleague, not talking to you as if you were a different order of being. Your client may be an expert and you may be a layperson, but be an *intelligent* layperson. Be someone

interested in a wide range of topics and who can understand just about anything if carefully explained.

"Barbara Quint: Grasshopper Searcher."
In *Secrets of the Super Searchers*. 1993

Sensory bonding with requesters has an almost sacra-
mental power to improve a search.

Wilson Library Bulletin, January 1987

I hate [*search request forms*]. I find them restrictive. They're
crutches—*glass* crutches; if you put any weight on them, they
crumble. They're mostly used in environments in which people are passing searches on to third parties, which in itself is a
very, very bad idea. It's easy enough to make a mistake when
you're the searcher who's talked to a client. Making mistakes
with clients you *haven't* spoken to is almost a foregone con-
clusion. I think that search request forms inhibit conversation, and the essence of my reference interview approach is
conversational. If the client is present and sees you filling in a
form, the process immediately becomes formal. You find
yourself trying to get people to stop talking about those
!@#$%@#$% keywords and start talking about their real information needs.

"Barbara Quint: Grasshopper Searcher."

… some [*search request*] forms designed for internal
reporting have sections for "databases selected"—as though

an initial selection could possibly reflect all the databases a good searcher will use as the search blossoms. You could change your mind walking to the terminal. The machines talk to you as you search and tell you where to go. "Now try this, now try that, and now try the other." How can you limit yourself with an arbitrary form numbering database selections from one to ten? How do I know before I start if I'm going to need 10 databases or 200? Let's see how it goes. I'm a grasshopper searcher, and I like it.

"Barbara Quint: Grasshopper Searcher."

Preparing for the Search

Before you go online, you should have all the factors and elements of a search in front of you, even if it's only in the front of your mind. This does not mean that the search strategy is complete before you go online. The essential value of the online experience lies in interactivity with the data. But unless you have a clear vision of what you want and why, you won't be ready for serendipity.

Wilson Library Bulletin, **January 1987**

The first decision you have to make is your basic tactical assessment of what kind of question you're involved with, what kind of terrain you're in, and what factor ultimately drives the search? … Does cost control dominate, or a need for totally comprehensive information? … If you're going for cost control, for example, you've got to shoot for the bull's eye, grab whatever you can, and then run like a bunny to get out of there.

"Barbara Quint: Grasshopper Searcher."

Actually, information possessed can be a serious handicap to the acquisition of information sought.

Wilson Library Bulletin, **September, 1988**

Knowing When the Search Is Done

The first criterion [*for knowing when a search is finished*] is: I've just run out of money. Ninety percent of the time you stop a search because you have run out of money. You hardly ever run out of data. But in the days when I had more unlimited budgets, I would stop a search when it looped back on itself, when I started reading references I had seen already.

The criterion of diminishing returns has value, but it is a dangerous rule to apply rigidly. Often, the reason you come back on yourself is not because the strategy has elicited everything there is out there, but because all the sources you're using are covering the same material. What you actually should be doing is regrouping and thinking, "Okay, now let's take another look at this. Let's look for a whole new category of sources—new subjects, different formats, different geographic areas, and so forth. Let's pick up those areas that *aren't* covered in the files we've been checking.

"Barbara Quint: Grasshopper Searcher."

Every professional searcher has secret horror stories about shooting past the point of no return to the point of insanity. The point of insanity in searching is when all the most likely search strategies have failed and now only the less likely strategies remain, but instead of stopping the expensive connect time clock by logging off, the searcher keeps searching because he or she cannot bear to have spent all that money to find nothing ....

Wilson Library Bulletin, **January 1990**

Searching is a gamble at the best of times. Play it by gamblers' rules. And the first rule of a professional gambler is: "Never throw good money after bad." If it just isn't going right, log off!

Wilson Library Bulletin, **January 1990**

Search Styles

I take pride in having been first to plagiarize Aesop's fable "The Ant and the Grasshopper" and apply it to online searchers. Ant searchers are careful, cautious constructors of search strategies, diligently digging through documentation for database details. Grasshoppers are just the opposite. Searching is surfing. Jump on the board. Catch the nearest wave. Ride it for all it's worth. Peel off and catch another one.

Wilson Library Bulletin, **February 1988**

Everyone who knows me knows that I am a "grasshopper" searcher. And this sort of thing, going down a list checking off items, is strictly for "ants." Remember Aesop's story of "The Ant and the Grasshopper" where the ant worked hard all summer, planning in advance and storing up for the winter, while the grasshopper played and sang only to shiver in the cold until the ant showed mercy and shared its provender? Well, searchers are like that. Some searchers plot their searches out well in advance, conducting careful, detailed interviews, anticipating all the databases they may need, checking documentation, writing out all the terms, graphing the Boolean connections; then, and only then, they go online.

Other searchers just grab requesters by their ties and drag them down to the machine for a merry session of searching. They conduct interviews on the way to the micro, select databases while dialing, and whistle up the first set of search terms while putting in passwords. They consider using LOGOFF HOLD equivalent to cheating at solitaire. It's a matter of style. By the way, you will notice that the grasshopper ended up living off the ant with no more than a promise to change its lifestyle. If "grasshopper" searchers do anything diligently, it's usually reading magazines like this one [*Online*] where they can pick up tips in articles written by "ants."

Online, May 1991

Search styles are not genetically determined. They are environmental, adapting to different milieus. Many ants have become grasshoppers when serving a multidisciplinary clientele. Many grasshoppers order an ant suit from their tailor for those special occasions when they search particularly precise questions.

Wilson Library Bulletin, February 1988

Remember, online searching is a lot like sticking one's hands down a pipe and feeling for answers with fingertips. It's not like opening a reference book and flipping pages. The data does not educate as quickly. You don't know what you have searched and what you have not searched.

Information Today, **March 1993**

Quint's Rules of Online Searching

- **Rule One:** Remember the bottom line when you search. Do what works. The searcher's style is not as important as the answer ….

- **Rule Two:** Stay open and aware and flexible while you search. Prepare for good fortune and bad ….

- **Rule Three:** Look for hidden agendas.

- **Rule Four:** Quint's Law of Research (plagiarized from a former client who probably adapted it from an old motto of a typesetters' union): There are three kinds of research: good, fast, and cheap; but you only get two out of three. Sometimes you get lucky and fall into the perfect search, but that is not the way to bet. Professionals play percentages.

Online, **May 1991**

Cost Issues

The cost block … should be a searcher decision, not a managerial one. Some libraries have been known to restrict searchers to cheap databases in order to get cheap searches. False economy! Nothing is a bargain if you don't need it. And no search is cheap if the results aren't relevant.

Wilson Library Bulletin, January 1987

Quint's Law of Usage-Based Pricing: Per-use is not ProUse. The minute you attach a charge to some element of the search process, the second the searcher understands that performance of some activity incurs painful expense, that is the moment you have set the searcher on the track of some way to avoid that charge. Professional searchers always yearn to steal the cheese without having the mousetrap snap their spines. SuperSearchers, a.k.a. R.A.T.S. (Rigorously Aggressive Trained Searchers), will always try for the cheese, later or sooner.

Information Today, July/August 1994

Of course this brings up the darkest side of connect-time pricing. When you get paid by the hour, working slow becomes profitable.

Wilson Library Bulletin, September 1990

The money you save today can buy more answers tomorrow.

Online User, May 1996

Every dollar a librarian spends these days comes out of someone's hide—the taxpayers, the research budget, the corporation (and behind it, the corporation's customers and/or stockholders). It is our obligation as information professionals to make sure that each dollar stretches as far as it will go in service to our clientele. The prudent expenditure of resources also serves the general growth of good products. It speeds the winnowing of good products from bad, good value from poor, by market forces.

Wilson Library Bulletin, **March 1993**

Quint's Laws: How Much To Spend on a Search

- **Know what you want:** Do you need just a specific fact or background information to explain the context? Can the answer come from any reliable source or does it have to be from *The Wall Street Journal* or *The New York Times*? Do you know which source carried the answer? Are you positive? Will there be lots of information on the subject, i.e., publicly owned companies? Or will you have to squeeze for every drop of data, i.e., privately held companies? Do you need to know everything about a subject? The last pieces of data always cost more than the first.

- **Know how to get the answers:** Time and money often trade off in online searching. The Internet may offer "free" or very cheap data, but locating the data and verifying its quality can eat up your schedule ....

- **Know how much the answer is worth to you:** Apply the "1776 Rule." In the last line of the Declaration of

Independence, the signers agreed to pledge "our Lives, our Fortunes, and our Sacred Honor." If you've got any of those three riding on the outcome of an online search, this is no time to get stingy ….

• **Know when to cut your losses:** Calculate your expenditures as you go along. If the answer just isn't showing up, jump offline and regroup ….

• **Don't worry too much about money:** Online databases still list among the wonders of the modern universe. Searching online certainly constitutes a simpler and easier technique than laborious manual research. The next time you groan at an online search bill or wince at going online for some information, just ask yourself, "But what price ignorance?"

Online User, May 1996

Medical Searching

Searching for patients has a last justification. Somebody has got to do it. And doctors do not …. The head of the National Library of Medicine has estimated that less than 10 percent of the nation's physicians have ever done or gotten a medical literature search. That is a real scandal—a scandal that is measured in pain and debilitation and fear and death. If health professionals do not regard searching medical literature online as part of their professional ethical responsibilities, then we online searchers have no right to put it beyond ours. Someone has got to do it. And let's hope that when patients start dragging printouts into doctors' offices ... health professionals will change their practices.

Wilson Library Bulletin, **October 1990**

In any case, the patient remains the ultimate decision-maker in medical treatment. Ironic, isn't it? The least informed and most emotionally pressured person is supposed to supply the cool critical judgment demanded in selecting and evaluating medical care. Nevertheless, it's the patient's life and the patient's money. That makes it the patient's decision. And that responsibility makes gathering information the patient's right and privilege.

If a literature search merely upgrades the dialogue between health professionals and their clients, it has done its job.

Wilson Library Bulletin, **November 1990**

Random Thoughts on Searching

I shall never forget a search on the ERIC database on how to manage teaching sisters and brothers in the same classroom. Out of the under-a-hundred references I retrieved, one sprang out. It concerned fish! On closer perusal, my search had retrieved a report on sibling relationships in schools of swimming edibles. To a professional searcher, that sort of thing is just an amusing story and an explanation for why there's a Delete function in your word processing software. But think how odd that would look to end-users, especially those paying document output charges.

Wilson Library Bulletin, **January 1995**

If you've got a question, online probably has an answer. But what if you don't have a question? What about the questions you don't know enough to ask? How is online as a "question machine?"

That's a different matter. In many ways, online information systems seem to dislike human curiosity when it's extensive. As animals smell fear, computers smell imprecision. And it makes them edgy, unpredictable, even hostile. Instead of appearing as a powerful resource, the vast bulk of online information seems a behemoth designed to crush curiosity. The charging mechanisms common to online penalize those who don't know exactly what they want and how to get it …. It is said that it takes money to make money. And an online searcher usually has to know something to learn something.

Wilson Library Bulletin, **January 1991**

When do searchers love to go online or love being online? When they've got a fun question with a fun answer. The grim-visaged price for accessing commercial online services often intimidates searchers from even admitting that online can be fun. Maybe the giddy Netters skiing around the Internet have made it safe to admit that even the three-piece suit world of commercial online searching can deal in whimsy.

Searcher, **September 1993**

Chapter 2

ON LIBRARIANS

Barbara uses the terms "librarians," "information profes-
sionals," and "searchers" interchangeably to mean trained
professionals who know what good information looks like,
where it hides, and how to find it; who understand what
their clients' questions are and pride themselves on deliver-
ing the best and most thorough possible answers. Since she
sees commercial databases and the Internet as unparal-
leled opportunities to meet users' needs better, she has scant
patience with librarians who think they can't afford them,
and who won't improve their professional skills by learning
to use them. She's been warning us for 15 years that librar-
ians who did not adapt could be displaced by commercial
services eager to profit from the customers we serve for free,
and as usual, she's been proven right.

What Is a Librarian?

A librarian is popularly defined as a person who works in
a library. Sophisticated professionals and a few awestruck
clients know that a library could be better defined as any
place in which a librarian works. Librarians make libraries,
not the other way around. Libraries were not created for

their own sake, but to perform useful functions in support of human needs.

Wilson Library Bulletin, **November 1993**

... a library is just what's left over when the librarian goes home at night, like a coral reef just represents the activity of living coral.

Searcher, **January 2000**

Modern librarians know that they could "library" from a phone booth if they had the money, the modem, and the micro.

Wilson Library Bulletin, **March 1988**

A library is a building and, as such, is accompanied by static verbs such as "stands," "is located," "contains," etc. A librarian is a person for whom action verbs are appropriate, such as "coordinates," "designs," "eliminates," etc. One illustration: libraries do not cooperate, librarians do.

Searcher, **January 1996**

During the first half of the millennium, the primary goal of libraries and their parent institutions is to archive knowledge. Knowledge is sacred, literally. It consists of sacred writing. Generously, the monks include non-religious and non-Christian material in their archiving, but all knowledge stored basks in the halo of sacred writings. The missionary aspect of librarianship is born in the archive function.

Canadian Journal of Information Science, **April 1992**

Archiving must never exist for its own sake. The monasteries are gone and the sacred writings dispersed. The value of information is measured in the minds of the humans who hold it. Measure performance by use and user. The first and last question for all information is, "What's it for? Who could use it?"

Canadian Journal of Information Science, **April 1992**

Knowledge is not a place or a medium. Knowledge is the light in a customer's eyes. All librarians should know that it's only data until you see the "Eureka" shining on the patron's face. Then and only then does information become knowledge.

Canadian Journal of Information Science, **April 1992**

Only librarians use any medium that works to gather any data that is true to serve the client. For librarians, it ain't over till the client is happy. We work for smiles.

Searcher, **January 2000**

WHY DO WE DO IT?

At a potluck gathering, I once overheard a stuffed mushroom ask a pasta salad, "Why did you become a librarian?" Quick as a quip, the librarian snapped back, "For the money." As a method of identifying the librarians in the room, the conversation was an instant success … simply tag everyone laughing—or choking.

Wilson Library Bulletin, **November 1986**

Come on, folks. Why do we do what we do? Isn't it because we like it? Because we believe in information service or information technology? Because we want to be part of the world's solutions, not the world's problems? Because we love to see the look of satisfaction or delight or stimulation on a client's face when we find the answer or introduce them to the Answer Machine? Isn't there a little missionary in all of us? Or am I all alone out here?

Information Today, **April 1993**

No, dear industry friends, most professional searchers have not made their career choices based primarily on considerations of lucre. This certainly does not mean that we do not care about money, but other factors have at least equal value. What other factors? Power? That one ranks about the same as money. A service profession would not top the list of the average job counselor's recommendation for control freaks. Glamor? My memory flashes to the look on the face of a top researcher I had always served over the phone when he dropped down to the library once and saw me pushing a book cart. Of course, pushing book carts was not my job. World quality research support was my trade, but I've never known an information professional who didn't spend at least some of their time schlepping. Safety? That used to be a good bet, but no job is safe any more—a truth that has been apparent for some time.

Information Today, **April 1993**

... the true function of information professionals and the institutions they create ... is service to people in need of information. This service mission exists independent of technologies. Technologies are tools.

Searcher, **April 1999**

To be fair, reference librarians were never really on the side of the library collection. Reference librarians do not serve an ideal patron with information needs that an ideal collection would provide. They deal with the erratic, intense, and variable needs of real library patrons. They always wanted to extend the library to match whatever the patron needed. With online databases, they can ....

Wilson Library Bulletin, **April 1993**

In olden times, way back in the 20th century, online searchers were usually information professionals. You have to understand—they were simpler times. In those early days, anyone who needed information from an online system would have to go to a professional searcher to get his or her answers extracted from expensive systems with complex interfaces. The searcher would listen to the client's problem, ask some penetrating questions, turn to a collection of online resources, perform some mysterious, indecipherable, algorithmic passes over the data, print or download the results, and present them to the wonder-struck layperson.

Information Today, January 2000

Many information professionals ... get praised by enthusiastic clients for performing ridiculously simple assignments ("My God! You found it! I didn't even know the year or title of the article and you still found it!"), then get chewed out for not performing the impossible ("I told you I wanted statistics for three Metropolitan Statistical Areas in each state. Where's the rest of Wyoming?").

Searcher, June 1995

On Librarians' Salaries

A special librarian told me that one of her best customers and most ardent advocates got a big promotion. Instead of wasting his "perk" chits on silly things like office furniture, he asked his executive assistant to find out how much a librarian would cost. The assistant came back the next day with the figures. He looked at them and said, "Is that all? Buy two!"

Wilson Library Bulletin, April 1988

[*On hearing of an enormous salary paid to a librarian*]
Golly gee, I can remember when librarians' pay ranges were too low to support any but anorexic headhunters.

Wilson Library Bulletin, April 1988

Lack of Respect for the Profession

Many librarians are somewhat defensive about their profession. My problem is that I can never figure out why we are defensive. Of course, people who respect only money and power despise us, but who the hell cares for the opinion of people who respect only money and power, the sort who have to kick off their Guccis to count their IQs? Come on! Librarians steeped in humanistic cultural traditions and devoted to service to the human mind need hardly credit the condemnation of the Yahoo.

Database Searcher, **September 1990**

Why do the citizens of the Information Age think they can get along without us [librarians]? Why do companies and institutions that special librarians have served for decades, even centuries, consider us ballast to be tossed into the waves? Where are they planning on getting their information after they lose us?

Wilson Library Bulletin, **February 1994**

When did the term "librarian" become a four-letter word? … What's going on around here? Some of the brightest people I know are librarians. Most crackerjack independent information professionals I know still think of themselves as librarians when their hair is down, regardless of their current job titles or descriptions. And even the dumbest librarians imaginable still take on one of the most demanding professional mandates in the world—the duty of answering any and every question on any and every subject, or at least starting the answering process, across reference desks around the globe. What librarian searcher, in half an hour's session with a database, cannot provide a faculty member with needed information that was left undiscovered even though the professor has studied the field for years?

Wilson Library Bulletin, November 1989

Sometimes the non-information professionals who buy our services—either as client users or as supervising managers—look upon what we do in wonder and then wonder why we ourselves don't seem to see the value of it. We don't price it high enough. We don't demand sufficient recognition. We don't acquire the clout and authority and responsibilities that our skills might warrant. We seem happy working in the background in a support function when our abilities and performance demonstrate leadership potential.

Searcher, February 1999

Professional Ethics

Librarians, professional searchers, and informationists have our own professional ethic. When we are asked questions, we answer them. Like doctors heal, searchers inform. If the questions cause us problems, we should work harder to solve those problems. As G. K. Chesterton once observed … "When you don't have enough hats, you make more hats. You don't cut off heads."

Wilson Library Bulletin, October 1990

More than anything else, a good reference librarian hates to say, "I don't know." And most would find it severely painful to have to say, "And I can't think of anything else." Vince Lombardi would never admit that anyone could beat his Green Bay Packers. He would occasionally concede that sometimes his team ran out of time. Good reference librarians can run out of time and resources, but they never let their client go without hope for an answer, without a suggestion as to where the answer might be or how much time and money it might take to get it.

Wilson Library Bulletin, **May 1988**

I've come to realize that it's my responsibility to make sure that nothing we do compounds the problem by wasting the client's time as well as his money. It's like the Hippocratic oath says, "First, do no harm."

What has always bothered me about information systems is that you occasionally do see them do harm. That's one reason I'm so vociferous about the issue of quality control. There are cases when [*people*] can actually come out with less information than they walked in with. Or they can come out distrusting the information they walked in with, even though it's perfectly valid. For whatever reason, if something doesn't show up in a database, [*clients*] may think the references they have in their hand are false.

"Barbara Quint: Grasshopper Searcher."
In *Secrets of the Super Searchers*. 1993

Why does clarification of sources matter so much to librarians and information professionals? For several reasons. In particular, when searchers perform a search, they like to know what they have and have not done, in order to assess what still needs doing. When searchers set up collections of sources for their end-user client communities, they have the same concern, but it's augmented by the worry that end-users will have less awareness of when something's missing. End-users won't hear that buzz in the ears, won't feel the hairs start to rise on the backs of their necks, won't smell the first faint aroma of fish in the air. ("Hmm. Funny, there's nothing here from ...? Wonder why none of the references are older than ...? How come all this stuff is in format ...?")

Information Today, **April 2000**

The only performance measures that count are client-oriented measures of outcomes, not production statistics of input. No matter how well and often you perform a task, if no clients care whether the task is performed or even know the nature of the task and its relation to their information needs, then what difference does it make? Statistics on shelved material in a circulating library are statistics on failure. If the material is valuable, why hasn't someone taken it away?

Wilson Library Bulletin, **February 1994**

Apparently, some people feel there are appropriate questions and inappropriate questions. I think most good professionals would say there is no such thing as a bad question, only a bad answer. And the worst answer is, "That's a bad question."

Wilson Library Bulletin, **May 1988**

Some searchers may find an ethical problem in "working for the enemy" if they have personal commitments to a social reform, or they may find certain positions on issues profoundly repulsive to them. As a person with a scattered history of activism, I sympathize. Perhaps my scattered history—one including scheduled meetings with right-wingers on Mondays and left-wingers on Wednesdays—gives me a unique perspective on protecting the process of civil liberties. I will search on almost any topic under two conditions: first, I will not use polluted sources. Debatable logic is acceptable; a pack of lies masquerading as evidence is not. Second, I will give the whole picture, not pre-editing to suit only one side.

Wilson Library Bulletin, **September 1989**

Years ago, a vendor representative at a library information utility told me that he worked at the company for a year before he came to understand librarians as consumers. At first, he found them terribly frustrating. They never bought anything fast. They watched and waited. After a while, he realized that librarians moved slowly because, when they bought into a product or service, they committed themselves all the way. After a sale, the librarians were on the vendor's team. They would work with the product, with vendor staff, with other customers. They would help make it better and sell it to colleagues. When he talked to me, he said librarians were the best market in the world.

Information Today, **March 1994**

Why Techies Are No Substitute for Librarians When You Want Information

Too often, the responsibility for high-tech information service goes to techies, lovely people, but usually lacking the professional training and experience to deal with issues of content and user needs .... In all honesty, sometimes the "bad guys" are members of our own profession, hidebound, stick-in-the-muds praying that they can reach retirement before they have to face the future.

Searcher, November/December 1996

In today's fast moving stage of the Information Age, a company or institution operating without an information professional is taking real risks, and, inevitably, losing money. Bottom line, managers might get away with getting rid of libraries, but they're crazy if they get rid of librarians. That's like going to war without a professional military force, or racing a car at Indianapolis without a professional driver.

Searcher, November/December 1996

Happy faces. That's what the new, cool online world needs. And making happy faces is what information professionals are all about. We define success in terms of satisfaction, not technologies like programmers or systems engineers, not sales or revenue like vendors. Other professions care about clients and work to their benefit, but they have other fish to fry. Look at a client trying to get a non-technological solution out of a techie. What do you see? An unhappy face. Look at a client trying to get a free solution out of a commercial vendor. What do you see? Two unhappy faces. If the client actually did manage to squeeze some data out without paying for it, you'd still see one unhappy face.

Searcher, **April 1997**

In the larger picture, who cares as long as customers get what they need? So what if we're not the ones to provide it? I think it does make a difference whether it's us, because only the people in our profession ... will do it as it should be done. We're the only people who have and always have had the knowledge that information is an extremely intimate product, that information is just data until you see the gleam in their eyes. The tool people don't have it. The industry people don't have it. The customers who don't know how information reaches them or doesn't reach them don't have it. They don't know how and when information becomes knowledge. As generalists, we are prepared to carry on an educational ... function.

"Setting Our Priorities."
Presentation to the American Library Association, June 1986

Why Searchers Must Educate Database Vendors

Unfortunately, most searchers do not complain enough. Professional searchers toil to create answers out of the raw material of online databases. They follow abstruse lines of access, learn anti-instinctive protocols, integrate data gathered through layers of varying database design—and all to produce answers to client questions.

Information Today, **September 1992**

Once again, searchers will have to lead the vendors into the light. Take them by the hand and insist that they listen to your requirements. Demand that they give you what you need, the way you need it, at the price you expect to pay. Show them your world. Show them their future. Lead them into the light.

Searcher, **April 1998**

Why should searchers—the information industry's customers—have to defend the product to the industry itself? Why should searchers have more faith in database products than their creators or vendors?

Perhaps because searchers are not the industry's customers. We are the industry's sales force. We don't really use or need or want the information ourselves. We just know who does and what kind and how much.

Information Today, **September 1992**

Come on, guys!! They're vendors! They work for us. We don't work for them.

Well, now, wait a minute. To be absolutely accurate, in a way, a lot of us do work for them. For decades, as intermediary searchers, we have turned their warehouses of data and their elaborate software command structures into palatable, focused, sellable packages of pertinent information for individual clients. For several years now, many of us have begun marketing their products and services to local end-user communities. Sometimes, they even let us do all the training and customer support. What the vendors do not do for us is pay our salaries or build up our pension funds or make out checks for our health insurance coverage.

Searcher, June 1997

And, by the way, a word of advice to all my sibling searchers out there. When trouble comes your way, do something about it. No one has the right to sell you data priced as a solution that ends up causing you trouble. No one!! Raise a ruckus! Call or message your friends and colleagues. Punch out any vendors who try to teach you how to fix their poor workmanship—on your nickel. Get loud and stay loud until the problem's fixed.

And if all that hollering just isn't your style, just send your troubles to me. They know the way.

Searcher, February 1997

And we searchers took it [*badly designed databases with poor documentation*]. We may have grumbled. We may have griped among ourselves. We may have warned end-user clients away from danger zones. But we took it. We accepted the burdens and the risks. The more hardworking and well-funded among us trotted off to classes or seminars, ordered extra documentation, read key journals. The less endowed among us held our breaths and dived in. What we did not do as a community was to draw a line in the sand and refuse to move our search dollars until key improvements and safety features were installed.

It's not exactly that we gave up. It's just that we once again let search services define surrender to their advantage. We let them co-opt our hard work and persistence into plugging the holes in their inadequate products. We didn't give up, but we lost anyway.

Searcher, **April 1995**

The information industry could profit by looking to librarians. (Don't just look! Hire!!) Professionals who follow client needs committedly build new sources of revenue, good customer relations, customer loyalty and trust. Two industries cannot afford bad reputations—food and information. Even the ignorant know that you don't buy information from someone who doesn't care if it's wrong!

Canadian Journal of Information Science, **April 1992**

Apparently [*information professionals*] have recently experienced a powerful surge of indignation upon discovering that throughout all the World Wide Web, they and they alone have an unbroken history of actually paying for information.

Information Today, **October 1998**

Perhaps we could lobby our professional associations for training seminars in how to be a pest. Actually, some seminars already teach those skills, usually disguised by code words like "assertiveness" or "negotiation techniques." The tune is the same, no matter the words. Basically, the lessons teach how to be a smart, assertive consumer.

Wilson Library Bulletin, **March 1993**

A lazy market that simply renews decisions made years— even decades—before does not promote product and service improvements. Lazy consumers make lazy vendors.

Wilson Library Bulletin, **March 1993**

Thumbs-down reviews will not help … new products to sell. They might, however, help them to improve. And improved products could sell well.

Information Today, **September 1995**

By the way, if your anger over a product problem pushes you into switching to another vendor, be sure that both vendors know the reason why the first vendor lost your business. The first vendor should have clear notice of what it will take before approaching you regarding reinstatement. The second vendor will know that it is dealing with a tiger—beautiful coat, graceful stride, but fully clawed and fanged. Realizing that your first vendor may come after you with improved offers, the second vendor has motivation to keep you happy in the future.

Wilson Library Bulletin, **March 1993**

This is no time for traditional or newbie vendors to rest easy—or to rest at all. To win or survive in today's revolutionary information environment, you have to move in the right direction, move fast, and keep moving. Vendors need all the guidance they can get. Louder, searchers! Louder!!

Searcher, June 1997

Quint's Rules for Negotiating with Vendors

Rule One: Research, Research, Research

Without careful and thorough research, followed by insightful, hard-headed analysis of the research, you may lack the necessary knowledge to engineer the best deal and lose opportunities for advantages you did not know you had … Collect the meat and potatoes research on product lines and prices for vendors and their competitors ….

Don't forget to analyze your own operations thoroughly …. A thorough understanding of your own needs will let you distinguish the desirable from the essential.

Rule Two: Make Only Win-Win Deals

Only make deals that both sides will want to keep …. Win-Lose situations leave the unhappy loser looking for another round or a way out of the game. Deals can go bad for many reasons, but they go bad a lot faster if one side wants out. Libraries traditionally form long relationships with their vendor suppliers. A clear perception by both parties of the mutual benefit inherent in the relationship will insure the smooth and unbroken flow of information service that marks good library operations ….

… Never appear totally unrealistic in negotiation, but let the vendor prove why you can't have the unattainable. A little naïveté can prove a useful tool in negotiating ….

Remember, the one who sets the terms of discussion often sets the terms of the deal. In any case, it never hurts to let a vendor see clearly and repeatedly what you would consider to constitute a good deal, regardless of whether you get it. Tomorrow is another day. In this buyer's market, memories of your vision and your disappointment should serve as research material for vendors planning new products and price changes ….

… Your research should have shown you what your vendor wants out of life … [A] long-range vision of what would profit a vendor can help you craft a deal that integrates your specific needs with the vendor's future success.

Rule 3: Look for Leverage

A good negotiator doesn't move without leverage and never stops looking for more leverage opportunities. You may not use every lever you've found during a negotiation, but you'll know you have developed the instincts of a true negotiator when you take a simple joy in just finding a lever.

… Most library vendors have begun positioning themselves for a life beyond libraries …. They need access to end-users. They need research on how end-users think to design end-user products. Trade that information gained from years of professional experience with end-users. Don't just give it away.

… Caveat: Sometimes vendors attempt to acquire their own leverage, for example, by marketing directly to your clients or your managers. Stop that fast! Let them know, and in no uncertain terms, that any attempt to backdoor you in your own institution had better work 100 percent, because if they don't kill you, you will certainly kill them. A vendor who attempts to push you out of the loop is not just an opponent, but an enemy. Against such a vendor, you fight with no holds barred.

Rule Four: Patience

You have lived without the deal for a long time. You'll live with it for a longer time. At least it will seem a lot longer if you don't make the right deal.

Rule Five: Keep Your Word

Honesty, as Ben Franklin used to say, is the best policy. Deal honestly and honorably with vendors as defined by the situational ethics of negotiating .... The information professional's ethical standard of Universal Revelation does not apply in negotiations. You don't lie, but you don't tell everything, either ....

On the other hand, once you give your word in a deal, you must keep it. If you say you will not share a confidence, you must keep the secret. If you promise to help somebody in a related matter in return for help with the negotiation, you must provide that assistance. Even if the deal turns disadvantageous, you must keep your word. A reputation for honest dealing is essential for making advantageous future deals.

Rule Six: Negotiating Is Never Over

No deal is ever really set .... An opportunity for renegotiation arrives with every renewal, or at least it should to smart librarians in the buyers' market information world.

… Stay flexible and stay portable. No vendor should ever think you live in his pocket. You keep your word, so they should trust your commitment to the current deal. But they should never think you don't monitor the market and study all the competitive alternatives. Worry them.

The Bottom Line, 1997

Threats to the Future of Librarians

Threat One: Being Incompetent

In case your library still doubts the importance of online database service, you might remember that at least four major online services (Dialog, Dow Jones, BRS and EasyNet …) have special programs to reach high school students. Ever been taught your trade by a sixth grader?

Wilson Library Bulletin, **December 1986**

[*I told you she's been trying to convince us for a long time.*]

Again, we cannot afford the waste of resources for preserving the status quo. We cannot afford to defend the conduct and standards of under-performing colleagues. Professional organizations must stand with the best against the good to try to ensure the future of us all.

Information Today, **May 1995**

[Re: the argument that charging patrons for expensive database services violates the principle that libraries should offer the same level of service to all customers for free]

Is it principle? The fee-versus-free issue? On the surface, an anti-elitist viewpoint seems very pure-minded. But when a service professional uses the unfeasibility of providing a service for all as an excuse for providing no service at all, doesn't that carry purity a little too far? ... I cannot believe in the logic of a service principle that results in less service, not more. According to that logic, a hospital that cannot afford kidney dialysis for every patient that needs it would solve its moral dilemma by pulling the plug on the patients who could afford the treatment.

Wilson Library Bulletin, **March 1988**

The honest goal of honest information professionals is to insure that their clients or patrons get the very best information feasible to satisfy their information wants and needs. If the library can provide it with the support of ... tax dollars, then happy is that library and happier its patrons. If individuals can get better information by adding money from their own pockets, then the library should still support them as much as feasible. Whether or not this means money in the hands of the online industry is really irrelevant. Pro-reading campaigns mean money in the hands of the publishing industry. What library director would instruct the reference librarian to stop pointing out the location of *Readers' Guide* when nearby carrels are full, lest it create a demand for a second subscription and make H. W. Wilson rich?

Wilson Library Bulletin, **November 1988**

Online databases are not a cherry on a library's hot fudge sundae. They are meat and potatoes, bread and salt, the five basic food elements. Without them, many questions simply do not get answered.

Wilson Library Bulletin, **March 1988**

Information professionals may grow defensive about their field when they face prejudice and false assumptions from outsiders, but, at the same time, many of us do resent and struggle against the negative qualities of some of our profession's practitioners.

Searcher, **May 1999**

The fact is that information professionals differ. Some of us are better than others of us. Some of us see the future more clearly. Some of us are the ones that the makers of that future should trust and turn to. The ones who do not see that future or who fight against it should not lead our profession. The ones whose resistance to the future stems from motivations that concern mainly their personal welfare and not any desire to benefit the clients that their professional ethics mandate them to serve, such unethical professionals should not represent our field. These last have gone over to the Dark Side of the Force.

Searcher, **May 1999**

For information professionals, the rise of the Net and its Web has posed a rolling cycle of career challenges, a cycle that promises to continue well into the next century. Some of us already sleep with the fishes in Davy Jones' locker (R.I.P.). A few of us have actually improved our lot considerably, finding life on the briny both profitable and invigorating. Most of us just hang on, firmly riding out stormy days in craft that seem all too vulnerable to heavy waves, but learning to enjoy the sunny days when the sea below looks as blue and peaceful as the sky above.

... Some people hope to escape the current's force by retreating into a safe harbor, though the prices on marina property, not to mention yacht basin rentals, rise steadily. These ancient mariners just want to live quietly with the systems and vendors they know until the Social Security Administration comes to take them away. They don't mind occasional excursions onto the briny, fishing for the unique, "ocean-only" catch they cannot get in their favorite seaside restaurant. But they scurry back to port each night as quick as their putt-putt motor will take them.

Searcher, July/August 1998

... there's the problem of "vision lag time." When information professionals deal with clients or bosses, they deal with lay persons, non-information professionals. Strangely enough, these people may often have a more traditional view of our roles than we do. They may perceive the "real library" as a brick-and-mortars establishment first, with some electronic doo-dads thrown in.

... In the past, this "vision lag time" may have given some protection to wicked or worried information professionals. They could continue doing their jobs in the old ways without having to face the future they knew was coming, because the bosses and clients were blind to that future. But the bill may have just arrived for not educating those clients and bosses, for not adapting and adopting the new technologies, for not telling the truth.

Searcher, **April 1999**

I want to know what the public knows. No experience in the Information Age is more humiliating for an information professional than to have clients using more sophisticated tools more knowledgeably than the professional. Look at the face of some poor branch librarian when a sixth grader walks in with more computer experience, or at the expression of an academic librarian from a small college with a new faculty patron who was just recruited from a university with integrated leased database tapes on its online public access catalog network. The librarian dissolves into a custodian of print instead of a full-power multimedia information generalist. If the great American public starts getting full-text searching using [*CD-ROM databases*], I want to know what it's getting. And so do you.

Wilson Library Bulletin, **October 1991**

Threat Two: Becoming Irrelevant

First, doing the best you can does not guarantee you're doing well enough. Just because no one could expect you to keep your library open longer than 40 hours a week or open on weekends or after hours without having to double or triple your staff expenses doesn't mean that customers don't want you to stay open that long. And these days, the Web's eternal availability, not to mention that of 800 lines and mail order catalogs, has made 24/7 (24 hours a day, 7 days a week) the new norm. Customers want it. Customers expect it. If you can't provide it, you lose.

Searcher, **March 1999**

… even computer support godlings offer day and night service now.

Information Today, **June 1998**

… We also know that too many information professionals still find themselves strapped to a world view, often not of their own making, that defines them in terms of specific formats and tools (Books = Libraries = Librarians). Too often the information professional cannot shake free of the debilitating burden such conceptions place upon their functionality and usefulness. Instead of giving information professionals the respect and resources and authority that their talents and knowledge and mission warrant, management traps them into sidelining high-tech solutions to problems as expensive extras.

Searcher, **November/December 1996**

Think of the changes [*the Internet*] will impose on institutions that have defined themselves by place features. One group comes to mind: librarians. We will have to burst out of the buildings that bind us if we plan to prevail in the new information world order. A good first step might be to rename our professional organizations to accurately reflect that the members wear clothes, not landscaping, that they eat food, not interior decorations.

Searcher, January 2000

Basically, traditional reference/research operations combine labor-intensive personal interfaces (a k a librarians) with collections of locationally restricted resources (i.e., reference collections), which users must visit physically or call, if lucky, at specific buildings during open hours. As accomplished and comfortable as this kind of structure may be to the lucky ones who have a good library and know how to use it, the model simply will not "scale" to meet the tasks ahead of us. You just can't get there from here.

Information Today, June 1998

In the past, even information professionals, like librarians, would accustom themselves to accept the limits of their own collections, or other immediately accessible ones (like the nearest university library), as the limits of their responsibilities for seeking truth.

Information Today, April 1999

The world of micro-service where one individual conducts searches for another individual is on the decline. It will pass into memory like the era when almost all cars were driven by chauffeurs.

Wilson Library Bulletin, February 1995

… As conditions have changed in our profession and the world around us, … conservative policies designed to protect the status quo have become self-destructive delusions. These days if you won't go after victory, don't leave the house.

Searcher, **September 1999**

A new generation of librarians and information professionals is emerging, people who may have different degrees than the MLS, who expect to operate within a broader range of career paths from traditional libraries to the information industry to their own companies, who consider making or creating databases as normal a function as handling negotiations for large vendor files, who work the Web before they use any other source. It was a joy to see all those new "Internet librarians." And, by the way, they come in all ages, because the Net seems to work on information professionals like religion.

Searcher, **January 1998**

I have not referred to online databases as a new technology. It isn't new. It's over 20 years old. That window of opportunity for the library profession has been open for 20 to 25 years. In my opinion, it will not be open 20 years from now. If we don't move fast, somebody else will do the job.

"Setting Our Priorities."

What will future libraries be after somebody else starts providing database access? The small libraries will be the lucky ones. They will provide testing rooms for technology. Come in and sample. See a CD-ROM before you go home and subscribe. Try out a database, try out a gateway before you go home and subscribe. These libraries will be the lucky ones. At least they'll get to see the world as it goes by. Large libraries, on the other hand, will be warehouses, depots where everything the advancing full-text technologies have not creamed off is stored. Some will serve as social welfare agencies with a rather odd view of appropriate décor for the homeless.

"Setting Our Priorities."

Changes in economies, world politics, sunspots and other cosmic phenomena may explain the motivation of institutions to reduce expenses. However, choosing to eliminate or reduce storehouses of knowledge as organizations enter a period of history characterized by general confusion over rapid change would hardly seem the most intelligent management strategy for any institution. Cutting information service seems to rank right up there with the decision panic-driven gunners made on ships under attack in Pearl Harbor in 1941, namely, that they could fire faster if they removed the gunsights.

Searcher, **January/February 1994**

Not to imply by any means that consulting or outsourcing firms have any endemic, systemic character defects, but—to use a possibly inappropriate analogy—when the rats start leaving the ship, it may be time to check the caulking in the lifeboats.

Information Today, October 1999

Executives managing institutions effectively these days must guarantee proofs of productivity from every function and department. Executives who support traditional functions without question will not be with us much longer; if they are, their institutions may not be. Librarians and other traditional information professionals can no longer hope to follow a strategy of flying beneath the budgetary radar.

Searcher, January/February 1994

Threat Three: Having to Retrain

… We information professionals are often jumpy, frequently frightened, and sometimes depressed about our futures. And, in that frame of mind, many of us may fall prey to the temptation to resist the future, instead of welcoming it (albeit with sensible caution).

Information Today, May 1995

No one likes having their knowledge and skills and equipment depreciate, but in today's information world, that's life.

Information Today, May 1995

In some libraries, online appears to have the same status as the Scriptures used to have in medieval libraries. It lives in chains, tied to the skills and presence of the ministering monk. Bring that online terminal out from behind that pillar!

Wilson Library Bulletin, **May 1988**

Information professionals must learn to change and change now. And whatever changes you make, whatever new skills you acquire or old ones you adapt, the process of change will not end or even slow down in the foreseeable future. Whatever you learn today, you will have to re-learn tomorrow. Whatever skills you adapt today, you may have to discard tomorrow and acquire completely new ones. No rest for the wicked and no rest for the service oriented in the New Information World Order.

Searcher, **April 1997**

[*Librarians*] must deal with the turbulent changes affecting their daily and future professional lives with an apparent ease, concealing from employers and customers how the rapid changes have left the experts as flummoxed as the laity. After all, if we really are experts on information technology and information industry developments, we should not be caught uninformed of the new changes.

Information Today, **May 1995**

Adapting to the new data sources will require searchers to engage in the activity they most dislike—learning new ways to perform familiar functions.

Searcher, **January/February 1994**

Hiding from reality is a sure way to catch it in the back of the neck.

Searcher, **November/December 1996**

How many professional searchers dread the day when clients want them to build home pages and implement organization-wide electronic publishing?

But don't misunderstand me. It's not just the techies, by any means. How many librarians at one time wanted (and still want) to provide books but not searches? How many searchers wanted to provide searches but not CD-ROMs? Then CD-ROMs but not end-user services?

Information Today, **May 1995**

There is an old saying in the information profession. I know. I made it up. "This is the Information Age. Are you in the Ignorance Business?"

Wilson Library Bulletin, **March 1989**

Once you're in the water, the choice is no longer between swimming and staying dry. The choice is between swimming and drowning.

Information Today, **September 1992**

… As Catholics are taught, there is no sin in ignorance unless it is invincible ignorance. If you don't know something, learn.

Wilson Library Bulletin, **November 1988**

Threat Four: End-Users

What are we worried about? Imminent end-user searchers. These days, it seems every professional searcher ends up looking into the earnest eyes of some poor soul who wants to get started searching. You can feel those round orbs, filled with childlike trust, drawing you in. Often, the future searchers are past or current clients. Should you not respond favorably to their starry-eyed plans to enlist the technology of the future, they will probably think your reluctance to share the searching experience reflects a desire to hang onto their business. If you're that worried about them replacing your services, then maybe your services are replaceable. In fact, maybe they should have been doing their own searching for years. In fact, maybe your salary or time charges have been a big mistake all along. In fact …. You get the picture. Of course, we professionals all know that no one is a better potential client than someone wading into the dark waters of online database searching for the first time.

Wilson Library Bulletin, June 1994

One way or another, you have no choice. You must respond. Librarians answer questions. Searchers reply to inquiries. If someone asks you how to become a searcher, that is a legitimate question that must be answered, no matter how dangerous the consequences.

Wilson Library Bulletin, June 1994

Look, we all understand that the Internet is an ocean. But most novices desperately want lifeguards, swimming lessons, and Mae West life preservers.

Information Today, December 1993

The primary goal of a search operation manager dealing with end-user searching should be to ensure that no one gets hurt, or at least not fatally.

Wilson Library Bulletin, May 1993

Time To Set New Priorities

Most of the following quotes are excerpted from an address Barbara Quint presented, in a session titled "Dollars and Sense: Implications of the New Online Technology for Managing the Library," at the American Library Association conference in June 1986, proceedings of which were published by ALA in 1987.

Database technology can convert any library, or library system, from an archive—a collection of possibilities—into an answer machine pushing beyond the information needs of any existing user community.

"Setting Our Priorities."

Too many libraries continue to operate as if online were an exotic and optional supplement to traditional library service. It is not. It is better. It is more comprehensive. It has more scope. And it is cheaper. How in God's name could that be interpreted as optional?

"Setting Our Priorities."

I have never accepted the "boondocks" excuse any more than the "underclass" excuse. The "underclass" excuse maintains that a library doesn't need good online service if it does not serve rich, well-educated English-language speakers. The "boondocks" excuse treats geographic remoteness as a justifiably invalidating precondition. Both are used as justification for inadequate electronic information support. A clientele that wants to get better-paying jobs, pass their classes, and expand their English language skills needs more information, not less. That eliminates the "underclass" defense. Remoteness is a minor inconvenience in the technological global village. These days, few communities are so remote that they don't have some cheap internet access. As long as you can reach a phone, much less the internet, you can get online. So much for the "boondocks" defense.

Wilson Library Bulletin, **October 1994**

Why has the potential for radical redesign of libraries and their services not happened? Money. That's what everybody says, but I wonder. I would like to challenge that it is money. Money follows priorities. Money is a decision to commit resources made by people ....

"Setting Our Priorities."

Sunset budgeting techniques will allow you to take a look at your operating budget, not in comparison with what your totals were last year, but with what your goals are. Ultimately, that kind of budgeting approach is necessary, because, when all is said and done, there are only two kinds of money—new money and old money.

… New money is what you get from someone who has never given any to you before or it's money from old sources but more than you've ever gotten from them before. Old money is somebody else's money. New money is carrot money, elicited with promises of benefits warranting major new investment. We have tried getting it for years with varying levels of ingenuity and with limited success.

Old money, rerouted money, is stick money. It tells the people getting the money now that they're going to suffer because you need their cash, that you've got better things to do with their money than what they're doing with it. A joint carrot-and-stick approach, by the way, is probably the best strategy, because without a stick you don't get many carrots in this world.

"Setting Our Priorities."

If technical services won't give us their money, if they want to hold on to it, they're going to have to earn it with something better than a mechanized replication of 19th century access tools. If they think library collections are so important, then why are they covering only monographs? That's a narrow portion of any library's collection—in an academic library, a very narrow portion. If they want to keep that money, I want every piece of material in the collection accessible, and that includes periodical holdings. And by periodical holdings, I include the full references for all articles within the periodicals. I want it all.

"Setting Our Priorities."

Public services may save a certain amount of money when online public access catalogs siphon off all the database searches reference librarians make to simply … find out what their libraries have in the building, already paid for and sitting on a shelf. With the full collection covered, the online catalog would qualify as a major breakthrough in a library's power to inform. Without it, those technical services budgets should be in trouble.

"Setting Our Priorities."

What matters most in the information facility? Décor or databases? Décor their libraries have, facilities they have, buildings they have and they can get more, but online databases are treated as an expensive frill. I work at the Rand Library. We walk on linoleum! We have no drapes. Our basement windows are spotted from the sprinkler. If we chin ourselves from those windows, we get to see dirt. But we've got databases!

"Setting Our Priorities."

What's all this chatter about building funds? Why all these plans for branch libraries? Let's look at branch libraries. First you've got to buy the corner, then the building, then a collection to put in the building, all of which is repeated in the central library.

Why don't you just buy yourself a really good online information system, a good control system for what is in the central library? Central will always have more than any branch.

Add online outlets for every home in the city. Link the whole town through the cable television system, for example. Put terminals in public facilities. Assign special numbers for businesses. Give a password to everyone who has a microcomputer with a modem. Attach an online ordering module to the information system.

Buy a motor scooter with a basket, a bookmobile for the heavier stuff, and—presto!—branch libraries. You could get a much better information delivery system for your money than building funds.

"Setting Our Priorities."

How many of you have erected obstacle courses that customers have to cross to get an online search? Hippity hop, hippity hop, two turns to the left, one to the right. It's like trying to get an address out of an information operator. And why are we doing that? We're controlling costs instead of answering information needs. The more ornate the design of the obstacle course, the better the chance that we'll forget that it is still a barrier instead of a gateway.

"Setting Our Priorities."

The Future of Libraries: The Promise

All small libraries, from whatever caste, should look on online technology as the Great Equalizer, rewarding talent and creativity over institutional investment.

Wilson Library Bulletin, **May 1988**

Now a librarian is a true generalist, an Archimedes among knowledge workers who has found the place to stand to move the world. No librarians with access to online information need ever refuse to start work on any question simply because they have no hope of success within their physical collection. Online data has created a universal standard for librarians. All librarians may not possess skills or tools sufficient to justify the expenditure of resources for any specific question. But any librarian with online access knows that he or she could at least start the journey to any answer and—with enough time and money and data access—expect to complete it.

Wilson Library Bulletin, **December 1991**

"Not Invented Here" is no longer a badge of shame, but a badge of honor. Find it, link it, and move on. Don't try to repeat what someone else has already done.

… When you succeed in bringing something new and good to the Web, then negotiate to become the supplier to others who need what you have. Never do something that's already done.

Searcher, **October 1998**

"The greatest good to the greatest number" demands efficient information services even when the efficiencies mean buying services you used to provide yourself, reducing staff assigned to old, familiar but technologically superseded assignments, and reassigning staff to new tasks that more people need done.

What new tasks would those be? How about civilizing the Internet? Or designing services that bring revenue to our organizations instead of spending it? Or creating information instead of just purchasing it?

If the thought of such daring commitment to new tasks out of the ordinary roles frightens you, it should. It's a scary world out there. Cling to the right. Follow your principles. They will get you through.

Searcher, **May 1995**

Oddly enough, however, information professionals may have a higher perch from which to start their climb to safety as the waters rage below. After all, they actually know what "real" customers want and expect and need. The wisest among the info pros even know how to distinguish among those three states—want, expectation, and need—better than their customers do themselves. (In the immortal lines of Angel Martin on *The Rockford Files*, "You and I know, Jimmy, you can't make one thin dime giving people what they need. You gotta give 'em what they want.")

Information Today, **January 1998**

Librarians should move quietly away from the tasks that no longer need our help to the tasks that roar for assistance. That Internet still needs taming. End-user searchers have grown into a mass market that cries out for protection from a chronic vendor failure—the urge to sell not what people need, but what the vendor has a lot of.

Wilson Library Bulletin, **February 1995**

More and more Web workers want and need quick, functional ways to reach critically evaluated, reliable sources of information. So far, they want and they need, but they do not expect. If they move forward forcefully now, traditional information vendors struggling to find new footing in the Web world may find a new mission and a new cash flow. If you do not, then the fierce competition among Web Newbies—search engine firms come to mind—and/or the public good altruism of government agencies and librarians may solve the problem in time without you. Help now or forever hold your peace!

Information Today, January 1998

What can information professionals do about it all? … Don't waste time or trouble trying to revive the dead past. With the phones ringing off the hook and management memos to cut costs stacked up in your in-basket, the most important task you perform today will involve closing a door behind you and staring at the ceiling.

Think. Think about your clients—today's clients, tomorrow's clients, all the clients who don't use your services today but should, and all those who may use your services without knowing they came from you. What do they need? What will they need? And most important, what trouble waits ahead for them? What problems will bad data cause? What crises has inferior data already caused?

Searcher, January 1995

In the future, librarians should expect that educating rather than retrieving may become the primary route by which the profession improves its clientele's knowledge, by teaching them to fish instead of serving trout almondine.

Wilson Library Bulletin, November 1987

Power shifts occur gradually, but they do occur. Online databases have a democratizing, egalitarian effect. In fact, if it weren't for the high prices they might even have changed the world beyond your recognition, bringing the average library patron service previously reserved for fully tenured professors working in major research libraries.

Wilson Library Bulletin, April 1993

For information professionals at the consumer end, two targets could seem to motivate survival strategies—making or keeping more money, and finding or creating more value. To achieve these ends, searchers could choose conservative or more daring strategies. For example, a conservative strategy ("Do No Harm") would reduce costs by guaranteeing that no opportunity to acquire information cheaper or to extract every possible use out of acquired information would be overlooked. A more extreme strategy ("The best defense is a good offense") would not merely seek opportunities to reduce costs, but opportunities to make money, e.g., by selling data created institutionally or finding new sources of revenue.

Searcher, January/February 1994

So how do you plan to learn everything that you need to know to stretch your online budget as far as it can go? How will you know when you are being penny-wise but pound foolish by avoiding an expensive but absolutely relevant database? Who will tell you when a file will fail? … Searchers are pretty inept when they search in isolation, unconnected with other searchers and information experts.

Unfortunately, online searchers have very few drums …. Humans who survive in jungles own drums. They network.

Wilson Library Bulletin, February 1992

The opportunity for being a Superhero, rescuing end users from dire perils … has burgeoned. On the other hand, the negative opportunity—the chance of falling flat on one's face in a public place—has risen equally. One way or another, though, information professionals have no choice. With more and more amateurs entering the information retrieval game, professionals must learn to leap tall buildings with a single bound just to hang on to their jobs.

Searcher, June 1994

Information professionals face the staggering task of taming the Internet, extracting and stabilizing all the good, identifying and filtering all the not-so-good, dodging the lousy.

Searcher, January 1995

You can't do anything right, or even learn how much trouble you're in, if you don't listen ….

Now that we information professionals have become the conduit for providing access to online data for our end-user client communities, let us never make [*that*] critical error. Insert feedback forms throughout the search process. Offer to serve as a backup to find any answers the system has failed to find. Find out where the information goes and how it changes—or should change—as it performs its tasks. Interview clients on their unspoken information needs. Ferret out the clients behind the clients. From the knowledge of the full chain of information comes the knowledge that makes better products and services. Only the customer has that knowledge.

Searcher, October 1998

Someday, some bright-eyed, bushy-tailed information professional group is going to get together and come up with a certification program for quality meta-sites. When that day comes, we want our site and our staff among the sheep, not the goats, to use a biblical metaphor.

Information Today, July/August 1999

The situation gets really tricky when the colleagues we see as blocking the way to the success, or even the survival, of our profession claim that their support for retrogressive professional conduct only masks their real support for inevitable future change. They know that we visionaries are right, but they know that current professionals find us too threatening. So these undercover radicals advocate policies that comfort the dead-of-head and lure them into supporting policies and practices that will, in time, expand and evolve into full-blown, futuristic superiority. The darndest thing, but right in the middle of your first "Harumph!," you suddenly realize that they might be right.

… We visionaries have to stand by each other. Sometimes, in the worst of cases, while seeking to maintain their cover, undercover progressives have been known to attack honest, open visionaries. Life as a defender of the faith is hard enough without getting blackjacked by your parishioners. So let's never, ever fall into that mistake. At the same time, no matter how impatient we open visionaries become for the future changes we feel must come—or even for recognition of and adaptation to changes that have already arrived—we must respect those who trudge onward, often dragging their institutions toward the light, inch by bloody inch.

Searcher, **May 1999**

The two goals of the profession will remain the same—archive and access ….

The name may have to change. The word "library" comes from librum, Latin for "book." Librarians are keepers of the book place. What new terms may emerge? Informationists? Information professionals? Informers? (No, bad connotation.)

Canadian Journal of Information Science, **April 1992**

Librarians can no longer survive, but they still may prevail. Tomorrow may not find them called librarians, but it should still find them pursuing their calling—the goal of providing knowledge to all who need it, the duty to defend the quality and value of information, the task of caring for the ignorant.

Searcher, **September 1994**

In all this confusion, in all this unrest, in all this chaos coming upon us, who will help people everywhere protect themselves from the dangers of inaccurate, overpriced, dangerous data, from the perils of relying on the unreliable and sinking into virtually baseless virtual realities? Librarians, that's who! Or information professionals, as we may call ourselves. As the old, but still painful, joke goes, "That's why they pay us the big bucks."

Searcher, **January 2000**

And as for that word of comfort, remember that the world we have spent our blood, sweat, toil, and tears upon has finally arrived. We were online before online was online.

Searcher, **January 2000**

These are not conservative times. These are not safe times. There is no hiding place, no time to rest. The only risk you can't afford to take is taking no risk. Dream it and make it come true. Move it or lose it.

Searcher, **March 1999**

Random Musings on Librarians

Mention AACR2 at a reference librarian's conference sometime. All I can say is, "From the people who brought you 'Bill-comma-Buffalo.' Okay, I am a reference librarian, though

I started out as a cataloger, but really, guys, how does this sort of author heading happen?

[*Barbara speculates on how it might have happened, after hours at a professional conference*] ... Over drinks and drinks, compromise works its mystic charms. The bonds of consensus are formed. "Bill-comma-Buffalo! Of course, why didn't we think of it before?" In the wave of good feeling, no one remembers that no member of the public will ever, ever, ever conceive of the inversion of a nickname as an authorized author access point.

Not even consistency justifies such an oddity. But in fact, catalogers are just as human as the rest of humanity and just as prone to the inconsistency that comes with the bellybutton.

Wilson Library Bulletin, **June 1991**

They say that no man is a hero to his valet. Well, no researcher is a hero to [*his*] research librarian.

Searcher, **January 2000**

... apparently the medical librarians would rather be right, rather see their clients get the best service, than worry about job security. Or maybe they just figure that, as a wise woman once stated, "We feed off of human ignorance. We'll never starve." Maybe they just want to get on with tomorrow's tasks and get yesterday's and today's off the agenda.

Information Today, **September 1999**

Chapter 3

THE INTERNET

To begin with, bq was skeptical about the World Wide Web, with its din of competing voices, calling it "cheap but flighty," which of course it was, compared with the quality-controlled world of scholarly publishing and disciplined, pre-vetted databases. And the search engines produced hopelessly vague results compared to the controlled precision of database searching. But as more and more authoritative information made its way onto the Web, free of charge, and as search engines steadily improved, she became both convert and prophet, warning librarians and database vendors that their choices were to adapt to this new model of service or die.

Not Quite Convinced

Frankly, the Internet gives me a headache. Gertrude Stein once said of Oakland, California, "There is no there there." It's the same for the Internet. Without doubt, the Internet constitutes the greatest success story in the history of electronic mail, electronic bulletin boards, teleconferencing, and even electronic publishing. It has over 10,000,000 users through some 500,000 computers on 5,000 networks in 33 countries and an estimated growth rate of 20 percent a month. What it does not have is a mailing address or a phone number.

Wilson Library Bulletin, March 1992

And then there's the Internet, that mystic force penetrating all our lives, the intoxicating brew that seduces humanity into the illusion that all knowledge floats free in an electronic universe awaiting the call of the needy or their friends and colleagues.

Information Today, January 1994

Is anything safe anymore? Are there no quiet backroads left off the Information Superhighway? Can a fast-lane stay-at-home find a quiet haven anywhere?

No. No. And No.

Searcher, January 1995

A Change of Heart

Wow! This Internet thing, this Web thing really works! It really works. And even if it didn't, it's so neat that I almost wouldn't care. Suddenly, it hit me in a wave. If I were young again (whoosh, there's another wave of ambivalence), I probably wouldn't even start to learn all the tools I have known and used for years to access information for fun and profit. I would concentrate on this thingamajig and let the rest go hang. I would figure that what wasn't in this doohickey probably wasn't all that important, or would be online soon enough to warrant waiting, or was too hard to find anyway.

If I were starting my career as an information professional, I would look to acquire skills to grow with—Net skills, Webmaster skills, networking, technical knowledge, electronic marketing expertise, information user psychological analysis. And I wouldn't call myself a librarian—ever. (Ouch! That one hurt.)

Searcher, **February 1996**

What did the Internet have that the consumer information utilities did not? Mainly, I think it offered a larger and better class of users. When you rely on user input to provide the data, as communication- rather than information-oriented services do, the better the user, the better the data, the better the service. On the Internet, experts talked to experts and filed piles of expert material into libraries of files. As for the user-friendliness, some of the experts on the Net proved expert enough and friendly enough to donate fixes. All the generosity created, and continues to maintain, a powerful inhibitor on price increases, at least those felt directly by users.

Wilson Library Bulletin, **February 1995**

The fluidity of electronic information produces an economy of affluence, not scarcity. I have electronic data; I give it to you. Now you have electronic data and I still have it too. Is everybody happy?

Information Today, **April 1996**

Initial press reports from the computer trade press seemed to indicate the computer industry behemoth might try to "take over" the Internet. Ha, ha. As if anyone could. It would be like going down to the shore and trying to take over the Pacific Ocean. Who do you negotiate with? A passing sea bass? You might try to take over leading companies in countries surrounding the ocean (a "Pacific Rim shot?"). In the Internet world, America Online has already bought up several Internet backbone companies. But how does that transfer into changing the character and flow of the content that drives users and contributors to the Net? No, the Internet is a force of nature, bigger than big.

Information Today, February 1996

The ultimate achievement of the Web phenomenon may become the transformation of anybody and everybody into online publishers.

Information Today, December 1996

… the distance between author and reader could vanish.

Information Today, January 1998

But the new Net-driven information environment is an economy of affluence, not scarcity, of open-handed liberality, not miserly money-grubbing. If people can't get what they want easily and quickly and very cheaply, they will try to find the information some other way. It would be rare for a vendor to have a product that could buck the freebie tide, and if they did, they would attract competitors like blood in the water attracts sharks.

Information Today, December 1996

Well, inchoate though it may be, the Internet and its Web have one firm strategic goal: world domination.

Information Today, **October 1997**

… the Web and the Net will never lack for reliable, unique, rich data content. The reason? Because people produce and distribute information for more reasons than remuneration.

Much of the data appearing on the Net stems from pride, a basic and longstanding human motivator. People publish quality material because they love the subject, because they want to show off all the work they've done, and because they like the praise they receive from friends and colleagues. Besides, the need for remuneration in itself does not block giving away data for free. In the case of high-quality, reliable, public-domain data, taxpayers have already paid the big part of the bill for the data's creation. The same goes for funding agencies supporting scientific research. The cost of delivering the data is separate, in many cases, from the cost of creating it. In fact, wide dispersal of information over a cheap, popular, and attractive medium like the Net actually increases the amount of money free to spend on data creation.

Information Today, **February 1997**

Netters [*are told they*] just have to learn three basic rules: "Information costs," "You can't get something for nothing," and "You only get what you pay for."

Just two problems with these arguments: One, they aren't true. Two, everyone knows they aren't true. Millions get quality data free from the Net and its Web every day.

Information Today, October 1997

I told you, World, that online was the way to go. I told you, Information Industry, that someday this stuff would reach the masses. I told you, Techies, that someday people would buy computers just to make their modems work. I told you, Librarians, that people would expect information to pour out of a computer like water from a tap.

Information Today, September 1997

The Web has its limits of course. Lord knows that. Lack of archives, disappearing documents, self-serving reports, out-of-date information, etc., etc. But Too Small is not one of its failings.

Searcher, April 1998

You know the old saying … "You can have it good, fast, or cheap, but you only get two out of three." Well, the Web offers information that gives users three out of three—better, faster, cheaper.

The Web's structure and flow have changed not only what authors, data producers, publishers, et al. can offer, but what readers, end users, customers, et al. expect to get.

Searcher, November/December 1998

So let's look at this from a publisher's perspective for one moment. The publisher is spending money to produce a print product that advertises the superiority in timeliness of a product that makes him no money, but which he spends more money to produce. Hmm? Anything wrong with this picture? Not for the Web. Happens all the time.

Searcher, **November/December 1998**

Commercial publishers could resist ("Hell, no! We won't go!!"). Authors could resist. But resistance seems futile. It's like resisting the force of gravity when you've already stepped off the edge of the cliff. Too late now. For one thing, everyone wants to offer better products, and the Web not only lets you improve, it practically pulls a gun on you if you don't.

Searcher, **November/December 1998**

Anyone who has used e-mail, listserves, newsgroups, chats, or other virtual community tools knows that they represent a wonderful expansion of human outreach. As a byproduct, they have also revived the art of writing as a popular skill.

Searcher, **January 2000**

My colleague is certainly right when she deplores ignorance of key [*conventional print resources*] in any information professional—old or young. On the other hand, one has to admit that such ignorance has had an unseen benefit. It encourages, and even forces, all vendors into putting their data onto the Web. The thought that all data exists on the Web may be an illusion, but it's a self-fulfilling illusion.

Searcher, **April 2000**

Of course, the problem that has always plagued every publisher or distributor of information remains for new Net "publishers," too. Just because you want to talk doesn't mean someone else out there wants to listen. Just because you load it doesn't mean anyone else will download it.

Information Today, **January 1998**

The Internet and its Web have created a mammoth and ever-growing market of end-users. More than that, they have set a standard and established a pattern of information retrieval that will, in time, reach everyone and will, in time, forever change and diminish the function of print as a format for archiving and exchanging human knowledge. The change will affect all areas and all uses of knowledge—from the highest levels of scholarship to the lowest levels of Entertainment .... The Internet and its Web have simply become a basic way of knowing and finding things out for millions, with millions more waiting for the conversion throughout the world and throughout the years to come.

Information Today, **January 1998**

Chapter 4

DATABASE VENDORS

At first Barbara loved the databases that allowed her to find in minutes something that would have taken hours to find searching through multiple hefty volumes of Chemical Abstracts. *But as databases proliferated, each with its own complicated search protocol, gratitude turned to "What have you done for me lately?" Why couldn't the databases be more user-friendly? As editor of* Database Searcher, *she started demanding better systems and more reasonable pricing, and insisting that database vendors listen to their users. When the Internet created end-users who expected information to be free, she warned vendors they couldn't compete unless they offered substantial added value and created simple, intuitive search systems for end-users.*

Bad Database Design

To relieve themselves of the moral onus of a problem, the industry loves to send out notes that tell you what is going to go wrong and how to prevent it. Of course, the problem is that when you get the note, you don't have the problem, so you don't pay much attention. When you have the problem, you don't remember the note. What I have always wanted to know is why, if they have a search strategy that will fix the problem, they don't store that strategy online and execute it invisibly every time someone searches the item. That would at least work in the case of new and revised subject headings phrases.

Wilson Library Bulletin, **April 1988**

At a speaking engagement earlier this year, someone asked me what I thought about online database documentation. The answer was C+. What do we have a right to expect? Forward motion.

Wilson Library Bulletin, **February 1988**

… good documentation is no substitute for better systems. It's only a defense against charges that you led the customer into error. By itself, it doesn't solve the problem of making sure the customer always gets what he needs.

Information Today, **December 1999**

Lack of attention to client and end-user assumptions in designing search systems can deteriorate retrieval reliability to the point where [*clients*] actually go away more ignorant than when they arrived. Watch end-users check for an author with a full name on a system that only wants initials. Sometimes they think zero results mean there are no articles referenced in the database. Sometimes they think the author did not write any articles in the sources covered. Sometimes they think the name they had was wrong.

All these assumptions are errors. The latter two are the worst kind of error, the most depressing for ethical information professionals. They mean that the information seekers not only did not get the answer they sought, the answer system stole their question. And billed them for the experience.

Database Searcher, **October 1989**

For years, the traditional online industry has tried to convince a skeptical world that a massive collection of references, with or without the full text, must have the answers embedded inside. ("There's a pony in there somewhere.")

Information Today, **May 1998**

As a Registered Curmudgeon, my response to [*full-text documents online*] is, "About time!"

… This is so strange, but so common. Dialog has all these full-text sources and the citations to them, but they don't put the two together. In fact, with UMI as a leading Dialog SourceOne supplier responsible for two-hour fax delivery of articles located in ABI/Inform, Dialog is supplying orders to a competitor for product they have in stock.

Information Today, **September 1994**

Essentially, information—like food—is a product sold on trust. If users don't know where data has been and what it does, they shouldn't put it in their heads any more than they would put unidentifiable food in their mouths.

Information Today, **September 1992**

So let me just say that most full-text data available from leading vendors and information providers is slop when it hits the desk of professional searchers. I don't think that full-text search services or compiler database providers have any idea of the contempt and anger that professional searchers feel for them each time they have to choose between sending a client dirty, bedraggled, junk data or spending possibly hours of tedious effort (hours they may not feel they can legitimately bill) cleaning up the text.

Information Today, July/August 1996

Information industry players, clean up your act—and your full text! Spell-check every article. Go back and spell-check the junk you've already loaded. After all, as publishers roar onto the Web with multi-font, art-laden, current, gorgeous, enriched articles, the quality of your archives constitutes your only competitive advantage.

Information Today, July/August 1996

The problem remains that the commercial online industry makes profits and generates revenue from selling people things they don't want, search results that don't answer the questions asked. The "power searching" excuse just doesn't work anymore, particularly not with services repricing and redesigning products that force people to pay for the privilege of finding the right answer.

Information Today, March 1998

… Eugenie Prime, now head of Hewlett Packard's library, leaned over to me and whispered, "They're not going to give us everything we need. They're going to give us what they've got a lot of."

Information Today, **September 1997**

Instead of standing there and waiting for the inevitable loss of market, why don't the search services get together with some of these other outfits—government, ex-government, advanced software developers—and produce competitive products? Why do they just stand there in the middle of the railroad track waiting for the 6:45 to flatten them? You want our money? Give us as good or better than what we get now. Sell it to us for less money. Adopt new roles. Grow new markets. Take advantage of the new economies. Use the new platforms to find new customers.

Information Today, **March 1998**

Let's take one more look at Amazon. com. The other day a friend told me about a wonderful book called *Angie's Ashes* by someone named "Roger" or Robert McCork. At least, that's what I heard. Like the Amazon-aholic I have become, I jumped onto the Web and entered "McCork" as author and "Ashes" for title. Amazon.com sent back a heartbroken message that they could not find any such entry; however, they wondered if by any chance I might assuage my grief with a book by Frank McCourt called *Angela's Ashes*.

… A week or two later, I went onto DIALOG with an author's name to check the book files. I expanded on the inverted version of the name with the spelling I believed to be correct. Nothing. Upon exiting, they billed me over $4 for the experience.

Hmm. Let's look at the logic here. Online services that get paid when you find something—whether e-commerce sites, like Amazon.com or Planet Retail (phase 2), or Web-oriented commercial services, like *Wall Street Journal* Interactive Edition, have a vested interest in sticking with the customer. They provide sound-alike software to correct failed searches. They provide browsing tools that link purchase selections by invisible consumers. They provide signed reviews by visible consumers. They synchronize their interests with those of their clients.

Information Today, **September 1998**

When your system contains information that could answer a customer's questions but, at the end of the search, the customer emerges without the information he wanted or needed, you lose. You may have the customer's money or credit card slip clutched in your hand, but you still lose. People don't want to pay to search; they don't even want to pay to find. But a vendor may surmount the latter prejudice by offering honest, reliable, "a-bang-for-every-buck" services. These days, with a sympathetic, user-friendly model of information retrieval advertised everywhere as the essence of the online experience, the burden of making a search successful falls completely on the vendor.

Information Today, **December 1999**

Web search engines return masses of irrelevant data or send users marching down paths to empty or half-finished data sources. The lack of organization wastes time, and as we know, time is money.

Yet when users turn—with money in hand—to the traditional, well-organized archiving services, they find them diligently working away at solving yesterday's problems, not today's. To this day, traditional information industry players still concentrate on rendering print into online. That's a fine solution to the post-World War II information explosion, but we're two wars away from that problem. It's been solved. Next!

Information Today, **December 1999**

We hope, however, that such new applications [*as natural language processing*] never boast "untouched by human hands." Indexing unsupervised by humans too often ends up looking untouched by human brains.

Wilson Library Bulletin, **January 1995**

When it comes to allocation of labor in handling information, you want machines as horses and humans as riders, not the other way around.

Searcher, **May 1999**

Above all, traditional [*vendors*] are doomed if end users or even professional Searchers—a far more forgiving lot— start to think that ... database producers don't really want them to get the right answers, but just want all the money they can grab.

Information Today, March 1998

Bad Customer Relations

[*On dead and missing databases*]

Grief for the loss of a beloved file is bad enough. Failure to send out invitations to the funeral can increase the sense of alienation among a search service's searcher community.

... What do you do when you cannot reach the file you need? If the file has moved to an unfamiliar service, you may need to gain access and learn new software. (No! No! Put down that gun! Life is still worth living!)

Database, October 1992

Vendors must stop penalizing those willing to pay for information. ... But if database producers, electronic publishers, and search services really want to help our profession accelerate into the Third Millennium, they might try abandoning several marketing practices that could get us fired.

... In this day and age, information professionals remain the only group that expects to pay for information. Vendors should not try to squeeze more from us just because we haven't lost our wallets. Instead, they should recognize the services we perform for them in finding new customers for their products, in encouraging our managers and techies to add their products to local intranets, and in introducing our clients to the concept of paying for data.

… You can get us to help train and support your products. But if you want us in place when you need our help, you shouldn't charge us extra for the privilege.

Information Today, **May 1999**

Most important, getting ambushed by vendors you have trusted can make information professionals look like fools to their bosses. ("What's this budget increase for? You mean that new stuff we put on the intranet is going to cost this much more next year? Why the heck didn't you tell me last year before we installed it? I thought you said this vendor was a good guy.")

The more conspiratorial, *X-Files* viewers among the information professional community might even suspect that ambush vendors had set them up, hoping that companies would transfer money out of the hands of knowledgeable, value-conscious librarians and into those of harried, inexperienced [*management information systems*] managers.

However, I do not share such a view. Long-term malevolence requires a discipline and foresight rarely demonstrated by the rather myopic and impulsive traditional information industry. Nonetheless, the destruction of trust from ambush practices remains a threat to both sides.

Information Today, **June 1999**

As I warned you in advance, when it comes to judging strategies that attempt to force customers to use services they don't want in order to get data they must have, my judgment may not be as cool and objective as it should be. I can feel my hackles rising and my incisors itching for a jugular. The scent of coercion is in the air. Grrrr.

Information Today, June 1996

One day, you will finally discover a consumer who did just drop off a turnip truck, who was born yesterday, and who truly is as dumb as dirt. Whatever you do, do not take advantage of the guileless innocent. For one thing, it may be a setup. What if the sucker's wearing a wire? For another thing, child molestation charges can make life real, real messy. You don't need the aggravation. Sooner or later, the sucker will wise up and wreak a terrible vengeance. As Lady Bracknell said in Oscar Wilde's *The Importance of Being Earnest*, "Ignorance, Mr. Worthing, is like a tender bud. Touch it, and it withers."

Information Today, March 1994

Service-oriented companies start and end with customer wishes and expectations. Marketing strategies seek to establish a smooth, seamless front of benevolent competence, a "no problem" service level. Ultimately, they hope to lure masses of consumers into a somnolent inertia, which is sometimes called customer loyalty.

Information Today, February 1996

Listen To Users

Do you sometimes wonder whether every magazine, every consumer product manufacturer, and every politician in office has a survey somewhere in draft, in the mail, in our hands, or on file? How wise we readers/purchasers/constituents must be! How the world doth hang upon our judgments!

Not all the world. No online searcher runs the risk of puffed-up self-importance at the attention paid to their judgment. The online database industry maintains a craggy independence of mind, a peerless imperviousness to popular prejudice. The industry never bothers to ask about the search experience. Was it a good session? Did you find what you wanted? Do you need more information on the topic?

Database Searcher, **July 1989**

More and more customer support comes over the Internet. But how good is it? Well, that's another question. It's a little premature to judge at this point, but it appears that database producers offer better Internet service than the commercial search services.

It's easy to see why this might occur. Most database producers have long traditions of direct customer exchanges concerning product content and service provision that extend back to print product days. In fact, many database producers have complained for years that commercial search services expect them to supply support for dial-up versions of their products, but don't share any customer information with them. It's hard to conduct a conversation when you can't hear the other party's answers. CD-ROMs erupted so rapidly, in part, because the technology allowed data publishers to resume direct customer relations without the barrier of intractable search services.

Wilson Library Bulletin, **April 1995**

The "All Mouth, No Ears" search services that supply e-mail systems with no automatic reply posting for bulletin boards and no file transfer protocol support are hardly likely to abandon their "I-talk-you-listen" policies for a little thing like the 30,000,000 potential new customers the Internet might offer.

Would the fact that the Internet adds more customers every month than the traditional [*vendors*] have gathered in a quarter of a century of marketing persuade them to change their attitudes? Nah. (Am I critical? Am I caustic? Am I sneering? Am I ...? Nah.)

Wilson Library Bulletin, **April 1995**

However, when two-way communication exists, the Internet bulletin board style will often allow users to discuss problems with each other and sometimes with more knowledgeable staff inside a database producing institution. I don't want to put down the people in customer support, but sometimes calling database producers with an online search problem can leave a customer wandering around from print sales to CD-ROM techies to order desks—or worse, trapped in some voice mail hell where no "Punch # if you ..." choice appears relevant.

Two nice things about good Internet support: first, you get your concerns on record and in writing, and two, other customers can help by offering alternative solutions or at least by confirming the problem for the vendor. (Customer One: "Am I nuts or has anyone else had trouble with ...?" Customer Two: "Hey! Nuts to the squirrels who designed this thing. Personally, I always ....")

Wilson Library Bulletin, **April 1995**

[After a vain, prolonged effort to let MCI know about significant errors in its database]

There's a nice thick line between persistence and obsession and I'm staying on this side of the line.

Searcher, June 2000

Frankly, the absence of interest in customer feedback so endemic to the traditional online industry has sent a loud, though silent, message to online customers for years. The message reads, "Don't call us. We'll call you."

When you have to place long-distance calls, even to 800 numbers, or journey to far-off cities to attend national conferences, just to have a meaningful chat with an industry representative or file specialist, this tells the consumer that the vendors only want to hear about problems or needs in terms of their existing product lines.

No whims, no wishes, no vague hungers, no data dreaming. Only defined, cash-in-hand, known-source needs. But in the world of the Internet and the Web, wishes come true and beggars can ride.

Information Today, **September 1996**

It's the last chance this year for vendors to take my advice: Put users first! Here we all are, tiptoeing into the 21st century together, and what do my shocked senses perceive? People ignoring my advice! In fact, the practice seems so prevalent that one might almost catalog it as a bad habit, even a vice. Well, I'm sure none of us want to face our Maker or the Future with such stubborn villainy on our consciences, do we? I didn't think so, especially when readers consider my fabled talent for always being right ("occasionally inaccurate, but never wrong"). Ignoring my advice could lead vendors into next-millennial experiences so unpleasant that the special effects for the TV movie Y2K would seem like a picnic in the park.

Information Today, **December 1999**

The consequences of not supplying feedback forms for every search has reached beyond shortsighted, counterproductive failure to acquire critical information for building better, potentially more lucrative systems. At this point, it has become somewhat dangerous to the vendor. Digital clients, especially end users, have become so accustomed to vendors slavishly seeking their opinions and reactions that they may feel somewhat insulted and even suspicious when not asked. ("Why don't they care? Don't they plan to improve this system—ever?")

Information Today, **December 1999**

Suspicion protects people. Suspicion points out the weaknesses of a structure. Allayed suspicions win vendors confirmed, long-lasting customers.

Information Today, **March 1994**

Give us what we want the way we want it and do it now. Or else what? Or else next year, someone else will be wearing that white beard and the red velvet suit.

Information Today, **November 1997**

Bad Marketing

Recently, while investigating the acquisition of a major software publishing house by a major information utility, I found the software house had no lists of key management personnel, no CEOs, no board of directors, nothing but an address and phone number (and I had to drill down to get that!). Who's in charge here? Is this company being run by leprechauns?

Information Today, **April 1998**

Why do they hide the product? Why do they call it by mysterious acronymic appellations instead of a name that says what the file does? Why *Compendex* instead of "*Engineering Index?*" Why *INSPEC* instead of "*Science Abstracts*" or even "*Part A. Physics Abstracts*".... On at least three occasions, I have heard Dick Krollin of EasyNet tell assemblages of online producer and search service executives the story of ABI/Inform and Management Contents. In every polite way possible, EasyNet online documentation attempts to nudge end-user searchers over to *ABI/Inform*, which even Information Access Company staff admits is much broader and more thorough than *Management Contents*. But end users consistently pick the latter because the name of the concept they seek is in the title of the file.

... Why do they hide the product? Libraries still constitute a solid revenue source for many producers and search services .... With all their long experience with the library market, why do the online services not load their full-text title listings or even their bibliographic database print equivalent listings into MARC format bibliographic citations libraries use to print online and print catalogs and other collection announcement tools? With a suitable notation ("Available for Computer Searching at the Reference Desk," "Library Electronic Collection Only"), every library catalog could turn into an advertising tool for the database industry.

... Why do they hide the product? Why does a bibliographic citation that matches a full-text journal article available on a search service not automatically offer the option to supply the article? Why is the practice only beginning to catch on and so slowly? Don't they want the money? Why do the journals that are online full-text never seem to know it? Why don't readers see regular ads indicating how they can get to a journal online?

Database Searcher, February/March 1990

Advice to Vendors Who Screw Up

"I was wrong. You were right. It will never happen again. Forgive me." All are words that angry customers dream of hearing. And some customers have heard them.

Usually words alone will not suffice, of course. You must remove the offense by reinstalling an earlier procedure or policy. You must offer some compensation, even if temporary. You must take the hit and be seen taking it.

This approach works most appropriately when any policy threatens a vendor's long-term image as an "honest broker." When the word goes out into the marketplace that a vendor cannot be trusted, that kind of negative image can do permanent damage. A reputation for occasional folly just makes you human. A reputation as a crook marks you as enemy.

Information Today, **July/August 1998**

No matter how heated or personalized the controversy grows, never blame customers, particularly not in public or heaven forfend in print or digital archives. Loud-mouthed customers may brand you an enemy, while silent customers withhold their judgments or continue a benign impression. If the vendor starts issuing charges against the customer community, however, they can produce enmity where none existed and even make enemies of friends.

Information Today, **July/August 1998**

Vendors in Denial about the Net

Traditional vendors must accept the Web, or die a horrible death.

Information Today, **December 1998**

The Internet is calling the world, but so far, the world of the traditional database industry doesn't seem to hear the phone ringing.

Information Today, **May 1996**

In a way, the traditionals behave like American auto manufacturers when the Japanese invasion began. ("But,

but, but ... Henry Ford was my grandfather. He invented the system that put automobiles outside every home. If it weren't for my family, they would never even have seen cars. And besides, we won the Big One!! Didn't we?")

Information Today, **March 1997**

Traditional information industry players have missed a lot of turns in the road when it comes to the Internet and its Web. Most of the misses look rather ugly when viewed with 20/20 hindsight.

Frankly, one finds it hard to explain how the online industry could have missed so many opportunities to get ahead—to lead the new wave of online. The early visionaries saw the world-shattering possibilities of online information. They tooted their horns for it. But few listened back in those early days.

And after years of sweating and slaving to build footholds in niche markets, I guess they forgot their original beliefs that someday the whole world would go online. So when the world actually did go online, the pioneers were not only not at the helm, they missed the boat.

Information Today, **May 1998**

As data proliferates, industry executives fear the move toward a commodity model will prevail and leave them fighting for market on nothing but prices and features. The commodity model puts the whip in the hand of the customers ("We are not amused. Dance faster, please. Faster! Faster!").

Information Today, **January 1997**

The Web has lowered the cost, increased access, and shifted market share away from the traditional online industry. Anyone who isn't enthusiastically on board with that is going to have an increasingly difficult time. I think it will be a tough year for the information providers. I think it will be a great year for the content owners. They will see many new ways to market their products, to get revenue from their products, and to capitalize on their intellectual investment in creating the content.

Information Today, **February 1999**

Nothing looks less attractive than information professionals wandering around with a dazed expression on their faces, mumbling "Where am I?" The doubts that many information professionals feel about the long-term success, or even survival, of traditional information industry players often arose initially from the perception that these people should have seen the Net coming .... Why did we see URLs on prime time television ads before we saw Web products from most traditional information industry players?

Searcher, **October 1998**

Unfortunately, many publishers with established brand-name products have not fully developed their product lines or business models for dealing with the new reality of the Web world. Instead, they become coy, flirtatious, an online tease. ("So you want an article, do you? Well, how bad do you want it? Ooh, you nasty man. You can't have that article, but if you're real nice and sign my dance card, I will give you this article. My, my, you sure do want that other article, don't you? Well, all right, I guess I can get you that article, but you have to give me something for it.") Some publishers even make users marry them to get that darn article—they call it a subscription.

Information Today, April 1999

When in heaven's name are traditional online services going to stop portraying themselves as competitors to the Web?! And who do they think they're kidding when they say they're bigger than the Web?

… Right away, this package promoting LexisNexis Universe started hurling challenges at the Web. The cover sheet states, "Searching other Web services has just become an infinite waste of time." Oh, sure it has. Let me see. All those full-text reports from government agencies, international organizations, professional associations, scientific societies, advocacy groups, and corporations—monographs that do not exist as part of regular periodical publications—I sure would never need any of those. And speaking of monographs, how about books? One site, the On-Line Book Page, links to thousands and thousands of full-text books, all in the public domain (or at least they all were until the "Sonny Bono Copyright Term Extension Act" pushed copyright protection back another 20 years).

… Second page of the PR piece: "LexisNexis … adds material at more than twice the rate of the World Wide Web (7.6 documents per second vs. one Web page every 4 seconds)." …

There is no way that hundreds of thousands of Web sites, many of which carry massive collections of material on each individual site, can possibly produce a total byte count smaller than LexisNexis. And half as small?! Ridiculous.

Of course, I assume we are speaking of the so-called "public Web" here. If we include the entire Web, then the argument falls apart on logic alone. Unless someone has repealed Euclid, a part cannot be greater than the whole. If LexisNexis has taken all its data onto the Web in this Universe product, then the Web contains all its data. Sheesh.

Information Today, **December 1998**

We all have to learn to live with the new realities, but the traditional database industry and professional searchers should remember that we're in this mink-lined lifeboat together. We both constitute the "high-priced spread," the upscale market for online data. If we plan on having a future, we'd better work together to provide clients with the added value needed to justify the high costs of our kind of online.

Information Today, **July/August 1996**

Of course, the reduction in the number of competitors could simply mean the remaining search services are stronger than ever. On the other hand, "market share" were probably the dying words of the last president of the American Buggy Whip Manufacturers' League.

Information Today, **June 1994**

Am I a troublemaker? Need you ask! But if we've got to have trouble, let's make trouble between firms making good, challenging products and then getting topped by other firms with even better, more-challenging products. Let the ferment of competition keep consumers reeling from the dazzling array of choices.

Information Today, **March 1999**

How Vendors Can Survive in an Internet World

… traditional database industry firms may find their battle skills a little rusty …. Nevertheless, they were here first and they don't intend to be pushed out of the way without a struggle.

Information Today, **July/August 1994**

So what can the traditional information industry—and that includes traditional publishers—do now? … The trick now is to find out where the leaders will go next and cut across country to get there first. Time to cheat, guys.

Information Today, **May 1998**

Regardless of the product produced, information vendors should keep monitoring users for situations that lead to complaints about too much data noise or too much of the wrong kind of information stimuli. Battered consumers are a market opportunity. Remember, "silence is golden."

Information Today, **January 1996**

The strongest remaining cord to the hearts of the professional searcher market remains the ability to scan vast, defined masses of data sources in one fell swoop. If all I need to do is search one database, no matter how big or small, then I'll probably turn to the most direct source, which usually means a Web-based product from the publisher.

But if I need to search multiple sources, perhaps in multiple subject fields, as comprehensively as possible, then I want my Dialog, my LexisNexis, my Dow Jones Reuters—any source that can promise me quick, sure checking of a mass of sources.

Web search engines cannot promise this kind of access since their spiders tour the Web at too leisurely a pace. Also, the spiders will not climb over barriers like registration requirements, even those with no expenditure required, or Webmaster prohibitions against access.

On the other hand, lots of professional searchers, myself included, are just waiting for the day when vertical Web search engines emerge that will intelligently and aggressively pursue the content of commercial publisher Web sites, e.g., newspapers. As long as they can assure me as to what I've searched and what I haven't, they can get my business. End-users may not require such assurances to generate popularity for such vertical search engines, though Lord knows they should.

Information Today, **November 1999**

Strategy One: Improve Pricing

When new services introduce radically lower pricing for substantially the same product, old services must react to those changes. If they do not, they will push old customers into the arms of competitors, arms already cuddling any new customers out there.

Information Today, October 1994

If you publishers or database producers want to sell digital information in bulk, don't make the bulk a cow that kicks, make it a pail. At least with a pail, people can see the milk, hear it slosh. What do I mean by a "pail?" I mean a collection of answers, the true milk of the online users' world! Primary publishers should not sell journals title by title. They should sell buckets of articles. They should not define the articles that will go in each bucket before the user asks. They should let the thirst define the quench. Sell 50, 100, 500, 1,000 articles from a publisher's entire set of digital works. Sell access. If you want to get more money out of a client, give more value. Hyperlink from footnotes or to forward citations (articles published later citing the article in hand) and offer those articles at half-price.

... Of course, if you traditionals ever decide to start solving the Web's problems, instead of trying to compete with it or just riding alongside—well, that's a cow of another color!

Information Today, February 1998

... search services and CD-ROM database producers should factor in the costs of customer support, training, and documentation when they evaluate how many resources to allot to search engines and interface design. If you design it right in the first place, customers may not need to call you to figure out how it works. If you design it really well, you may not even need training sessions. If you design it perfectly, you might not even need documentation.

Information Today, **January 1995**

Answer-oriented pricing puts pressure on the information industry to reach the answer quickly and efficiently .... In contrast, connect-time pricing positively rewards system ineptitude.

Database Searcher, **May 1991**

No Stupidity Fees ... I was sick and tired of any system charging me for searching in any form. I came to this system for answers, and answers were the only thing I wanted to pay for.

Information Today, **November 1998**

[*On an expensive, fruitless search*]
$84.14 is answer money, not citation money.

Information Today, **October 1994**

Multiple Payment Options: Here we go again with the same old message. Take the money! Take the money! Take the money!

Information Today, **November 1998**

Here's a wild and wooly scheme: Guarantee your clients that your service will always offer the best price. We see those kinds of promises regularly everywhere, from consumer electronics establishments to car dealerships. ("Our prices cannot be beat! If you can find it cheaper elsewhere, we will refund the difference.") How about building a system that tracks full text sources on the Web and takes users to the cheapest source?

Why would you want to do that? Because when librarians build 24-hour, round-the-clock services … they will need vendors who will supply the same client-oriented, budget-wary service the librarians would supply for walk-in clients. Because librarians can sell their end-user managers on that kind of vendor. Because that kind of service with that kind of commitment is one that librarians, their clients, and their managers could trust in the dark.

Information Today, June 1998

Even the people who have the skills and the resources to pay the top-dollar prices that the traditional database industry charges have come to feel that they have the absolute right to insist on comfort for their cash. After all, what kind of world has the champagne and plumped pillows going to coach class, while first class passengers just get a map to the galley refrigerator and a cheat sheet on how to use the microwave?

Information Today, June 1997

However, if LexisNexis treats the new product as a loss leader designed to generate customer contacts to whom they can then market "real" online with "real" search software features for "real" money, well, like they say, that dog won't hunt. No consumer smart enough to read his or her own name on a credit card is going to go from $30 a month for information to $30 a search or $100 or $200 or $400 an hour. Try to sell the idea and the words "bait-and-switch" and "ice skating in hell" will fill the air.

Information Today, July/August 1997

Strategy Two: Archive the Web

The problem that has most information professionals and Web workers pulling their hair out these days involves the evanescent nature of useful material carried on and/or identified through the Web. The good stuff comes and goes with barely a trace or a note "to whom it may concern."

Print sources, whether retrieved digitally or through old-fashioned manual research, compound the problem. Scholarly reports, trade press articles, national newspaper items, popular magazine pieces—all cite Web pages as though the Web were cast in stone. In many cases, readers of print will be lucky if the cited sites and their content have not vanished before they finish reading the material clutched in their hands.

Information Today, November 1997

Why in heaven's name full-text services have not pursued the raw material of listservs and newsgroups and Web site archiving, material so raw that they could actually generate print as well as online products from it, I will never know. Most of my current theories for the omission would not compliment industry executives. The words "lazy lem-mings" and "not-a-risk-taker-in-a-carload" come to mind.

Information Today, December 1996

If the traditional search services and data aggregators have any hope of survival, they must find a way to turn the disintermediation effect of the Net and its Web to their advantage. They must find a way to get to new sources before their competitors (or "coopetitors") do.

Archiving e-zines, Webzines, listserv content, and what-ever else of solid value they can find on the Net gives them a chance to form new, productive relationships with sources. Most of these sources still have major problems with archiving. Even if an individual site has committed itself religiously to meticulous archiving, it can still only archive its own material. Search services and aggregators can supply users with a way to scan hundreds and thou-sands of archives in one smooth step.

Please, please stop slicing and dicing what you've got and get new material! Stop adding some print title everyone else has just because everyone else has it! Stop considering your competition as the guys in the exhibit booth across the aisle from you at some industry conference! The enemy is outside; it's in the alternatives to your entire approach to information. The opportunity lies in solving new problems and using those solutions to reach whole new markets in new ways.

Information Today, December 1999

More opportunities await friends of the Web .... Distance learning has become more and more a reality as both traditional colleges and universities and Avis-like (number-two-but-trying-harder) educational institutions expand their services using the Net. Extranets combine subsets of proprietary, internal information with integrated access to external information sources, and offer the combination to privileged clients or suppliers. Partnering with such efforts should constitute a natural opportunity for the traditionals to make their controlled, known-content collections serve as digital libraries.

Information Today, **December 1998**

So what [*else*] can traditionals do to recapture momentum in the new Web-oriented marketplace? How about turning to a previously ignored literature: books? ...

First, there are the in-print books that have electronic versions, like 1,350 titles from the National Academy Press (http://www.nap.edu). Look those titles up in Books in Print and you'll find them listed, but will you find their Web URLs? I don't think so. For all intents and purposes, those books sit waiting on a virtual bookshelf for any librarian or library patron to access, if we know about them ....

Second, there are all those luscious, full-text, public domain books, typified by Project Gutenberg's historic collection. Whole meta-sites are devoted to locating public domain books .... These sources represent a free virtual bookshelf, or bookcase or small library, available for librarians and their library patrons. In the case of many public domain titles, like those accumulated by Project Gutenberg, ignorance of this content amounts to losing a set of the Great Books of the Western World.

Third, there are all the new electronic only books sneaking onto the Web .... In effect, Fatbrain [*a Web service that allows authors to post their books for download and splits revenues evenly with authors*] and the Web replace publishers. Considering the meager royalties publishers pay book authors, this option could have a lot of appeal.

Well, here we don't have the crisis of missing freebies, but of missing books altogether. Librarians really hate to think that a whole body of book/monograph literature is growing bigger and bigger everyday, while they have no way of knowing about it, except by checking each electronic publisher's individual catalog ....

Then there are all the other sales opportunities. After all, all these electronic books are available, either for sale or for downloading. A service that indexed all the electronic books available would have new e-commerce options open for generating revenue. They could get a percentage on any book order placed online, just like a bookstore or Amazon.com. Opportunities would exist even in the area of public domain: downloadable books. Many people who look at an online book find that they prefer to read it in print. So how about getting them a print copy? Make a deal with Kinko's or some other service to produce bound books. In fact, you could customize the books' cover pages with unique input and have them shipped to users. Or find existing print copies, e.g., with Amazon.com or barnesandnoble.com, and offer them for direct delivery.

Strategy Three: Create New Content

Let's leap ahead. Create original and exclusive material for the Web site. ("Content is God.") Identify questions people ask and material that answers all or part of those questions. Calculate the level of interest. Forecast how long it will last. Contract with the authors who write the articles to maintain those articles—current and complete (including supplementary material and links)—for a period of time.

Information Today, **May 1998**

Strategy Four: Add Value

We hear every day about the wonder and necessity of "Value-Added," how it makes all products sell, how it underlies winning corporate strategies. Strangely enough for the lyricists of management fads, in this case, all the claims appear to be true. Not the claims as applied to specific situations, companies, products, or services, of course. (Let us not abandon the lessons of universal human experience quite that quickly.) But when you look at winning strategies, winning products, and winning services, you do tend to notice Value-Added peeking back at you.

Information Today, **September 1996**

Before the search services and database producers engage in dramatically different Value-Added projects, they should probably try to eliminate the practice of throwing away the good stuff they already have.

Project One: Identify the good. Protect it from destruction. Share the news about the good stuff and its uses with clients and customers ....

Project Two: Analyze the good. Figure out what would make it work better. Identify what information or connections not currently acquired would complement what you already have. Acquire, develop, and add the new material or connections. Share the good news about the better stuff and its uses with clients and customers.

Information Today, September 1996

More than that, if traditional online services could supply the critical eyes to distinguish the good from the bad and the best from the good, if they could take over the editorial role of evaluating, checking, and improving material before they archived it, then they could find the Internet a sea of publishing opportunities.

Information Today, May 1998

In May [1997], *Business Week* published a special report on emerging virtual communities that had a fascinating statistic. Apparently, the average stay for a serious Web visit—the computation eliminated stays of less than a few seconds—lasts seven minutes. When a Web site adds a "chat" feature, the average duration jumps to 30 minutes.

That's a big difference. It's a difference that makes a difference. Advertisers should like it. Phone companies may abhor it. Information firms should not ignore it. If people use your information in communicating with others, maybe they should do so without leaving your venue. That way, your old customers could bring in new customers. "Word of keyboard?"

Information Today, November 1997

Strategy Five: Follow Quint's Rules for the Perfect Information Portal

Rule One: Build a portal that works as comfortably and as effortlessly as possible. Do not rely on the sophistication of information professional users to compensate for inadequate, incomplete Web designs. To this day, many traditional online services stick users with the burden of handling everyday programming tasks every time they fire up their systems. It's a bad habit, one information professionals have come to resent more and more as they see the love and kisses given to end-users.

Rule Two: Move the mountain (of data), not Mohammed. Overall, the site should offer layers of approaches based on a triple taxonomy—user experience (novice, expert, manager), field of interest (business, sci-tech, social sciences/arts/humanities), and vendor resources. Each page or piece of information added to the site would be categorized using this taxonomy.

Rule Three: Feedback, feedback, feedback—the PIP [*Perfect Information Portal*] should bubble and boil with communication. The portal should constantly promote input from users—input to the portal and its designers on how to improve the product, reactions to news announcements synthesized and recorded for latecomers, feedback to vendors on problems or opportunities in their products and services, tips to the portal designers on current user concerns, etc. We want the PIP to be the first place to which information professionals on both sides of the screen—customers and vendors—turn for full background information and for fast-breaking developments.

Information Today, **February 2000**

To succeed and endure, a good portal must build a firewall between editorial content and advertiser interests.

Information Today, **February 2000**

So who's going to pay for [*PIP*]? Right off the bat, not the user. If the Web has taught us any general economic truths, it is that charging users for using just doesn't work.

To succeed, portals need "mindshare." They need the broadest possible base of users in their target market. They need to dominate their field. That means avoiding the construction of any barriers to acquiring new users, and no barrier stops the flow faster than billing.

Some commentators keep hoping that the old habits of paying for what you use will return and infect the Web. Sorry. That's not like waiting for the swallows to come back to Capistrano; it's more like waiting for the horse to replace the automobile. Ain't gonna happen!

Information Today, **February 2000**

Strategy Six: Appeal to End-Users

Whatever course information industry executives take, let me suggest one absolutely necessary direction: Head for the customers. Find out what they want. Ask them. Listen. Change.

If you can do it together with other firms, that could accelerate the change process for the whole industry. And, frankly, the great challenge you face today is not fighting for market share with your old, familiar rivals. That's like arguing about tomorrow's shuffleboard schedule while they're lowering the lifeboats. The entire industry faces a survival challenge from revolutionary new technologies and the revolution of rising user expectations. Move it or lose it!

Information Today, January 1997

Problem: Big trouble here, guys. I have yet to see an end-user interface from a traditional information industry vendor that did not require a college diploma at least. Usually they require post-graduate work. Users must come to the site already knowing key sources, bibliographic structure, grammar, linguistics, Boolean logic, etc. If they do not arrive with these skills in place, they better prove astonishingly intuitive students or prepare to spend hours studying help screens and manuals.

Basically, the traditional services seem to design end-user systems with no help from any real end users. Instead of studying how "real people" look for information and constructing their interfaces to accommodate those patterns, they treat end users as suppliants who will simply have to learn to ask proper questions in a proper manner, before they can get what passes for answers.

Information Today, October 1997

Systems should learn about users, not users about systems.
Information Today, November 1998

How rich we all would be if we had a nickel for every time we saw someone sit down at a computer terminal in a high-tech thriller and proceed to type English language questions into a machine.
Wilson Library Bulletin, March 1994

If there's any lesson computer development has taught over the last decade or more, it is that people just want to do it, they don't want to learn it.
Information Today, November 1998

Users have too much to do and learn in their regular lives to waste their time learning how to help vendors deliver promised information.
Information Today, June 1997

Real end users ... have been coddled by customer-friendly software all their computer lives. As a rule, the limited time and effort and money end users devote to computer-assisted tasks must produce heavy dividends or they will simply go without. And that rule grows in force. The newer the user, the lower the pain threshold.
Information Today, January 1995

Don't imprison data in paradigms built around your production problems. Users just don't care. Library catalogers and bibliographic indexers invert authors' names because it once made it easier to file in printed catalogs or indexes. So what? Computer users don't have that problem. If they enter a name un-inverted, the system should accept it.

Information Today, **November 1998**

How do WordPerfect and other software developers get away with it? First, they identify what customers want to do most of the time and how they want to do it—the old 80/20 rule (people use 20 percent of a program's functions 80 percent of the time). Good software developers make high-use functions as simple and automatic and inevitable as possible.

Information Today, **January 1995**

The standards for basic functionality have changed as the Web's growth has redefined online as the newest of the mass media. No longer can a vendor get by with "possibility" or even "feasibility" as proof of success in claiming a feature for their product; ease is everything. In the realm of software, they call it OOBE (rhymes with newbie)—the out-of-box experience.

If the purchaser can't slit the cardboard on the CD-ROM case, slide the disk out of the folder, fling it into the drive, and start the installation in one fluid, unbroken motion, forget it! The vendor has failed the usability test, and no amount of make-up homework will ever lift their grade above a "C-minus."

Information Today, **September 1998**

Now how many amateur searchers are going to realize that entering the term "dog" won't even retrieve "dog**s**," much less "spaniels, poodles, terriers, etc.?" You must give end-users a system that compensates for their lack of skills in its search interfaces and protects their budgets with reduced pricing, while not denying them access to the best and broadest array of data.

Wilson Library Bulletin, **June 1994**

New miracle products and services usually try to cross the "Loathing for Learning" barrier with one of two approaches. Either they attempt to anticipate user ineptitude and preconfigure the system to operate within its limits (e.g., ATMs, Federal Express, etc.). Or they try to convert users into a new class of experts, enthusiastic and diligent in the pursuit of the opportunity to be insufferably superior to all non-experts.

Wilson Library Bulletin, **December 1994**

Exclusivity still has a *raison d'etre*. Inelegance, however, is doomed. In the world of end-user searching that continues to grow exponentially, inelegance is fatal.

We all learn that lesson from personal experience by searching and surfing the Web. Frankly, it's "out of sight, out of mind" for end-user searchers. If you cannot shove your product into their line of sight, they won't go hunting for it more than a moment or two. If they feel any hitches or glitches in accessing your products, they won't stay more than a few minutes. After all, they're not like professional searchers. They have lives.

Information Today, **December 1996**

To insure the long life and comfort of your searchers, try to pick an interface that meets "Quint's 20/20 Rule." That means a system that does a lot of what you bought it to do within 20 minutes after you start using it, but a lot more after you've used it for 20 days.

Wilson Library Bulletin, **December 1986**

Patrons want answers, not references. When they pay for their own computer searches, they really want answers. Every computer on television or in the movies has full answers. So why don't you?

Wilson Library Bulletin, **November 1986**

People want what they want before they want what they need, and what they want first is what a free market gives them first.

Database Searcher, **September 1992**

Market is not defined by what the vendor sells but what the customer buys.

Information Today, **June 1994**

End users are a fickle lot. If they see something bright and shiny and cheap, they will wander away from established services. After all, they don't have to be reasonable or industrious to be right. They're the customers. They're born right.

Information Today, **March 1996**

At this point, Dow Jones' only competition for ease of use comes not from a traditional competitor, but from a Net newbie. Northern Light makes it just as easy to pay, has no annual fee, and offers a free Web search engine. However, Northern Light doesn't have the content Dow Jones does.

Notice, however, that that fact has not stopped Northern Light from becoming a competitor. I told you those Web searchers were lazy.

Information Today, **April 1999**

What do Web workers require? First, they require one-stop shopping. They want the whole answer in one search session.

Information Today, **September 1997**

The point about mass consumer marketing is to encourage conspicuous consumption. Don't buy things because you need them. Buy things because you want them. [*Those*] who want information on a disease because they have the condition and don't want to suffer or die, may pay a professional searcher a hefty fee to acquire the information. Someone who just wants to check the veracity of last night's "Disease of the Week" movie to settle a bet with another television watcher, won't. However, the information industry has the opportunity for two sales here, not one, if it can provide attractive pricing.

Information Today, **January 1994**

More and more people are dealing with more and more data every day. The question is not whether the market is big enough for a supermarket search service. The question is whether the supermarket search service is big enough for the market.

Information Today, June 1994

However, potential new customers have lived without your product till now and have no reason not to think they could live without it in the future. With primitive life forms, suspicion and inertia go hand in hand.

Information Today, March 1994

Search services and full-text compiler database producers still structure their source selections around what libraries carry. If traditional database vendors want to acquire new, exclusive sources, they should look beyond library-selection criteria. For one thing, they should dump the "goody-two-shoes" effect of mirroring library selection policies.

… I recall once starting a tempest in a teapot at a company where I used to work when I tried to integrate a list of journals available through our full-text online services with a list of the library's print subscription holdings. IAC had just added *Playboy* magazine. When the subscription holdings list went out to the company staff, the head librarian nearly had a hernia snatching back copies of the list and ordering its revision to excise the "shocking" title. Of course, I tried to tell her that in the commercial online of that day, you really, really only read *Playboy* for the articles ("ASCII: The Bowdler Effect").

Information Today, December 1996

There are a lot of high-circulation, long-established periodicals out there that do not have any coverage in traditional online full-text archive services, apparently because they describe areas of human interest not approved by every American or, at least, not every 19th-century American.

… How about psychic phenomena and the occult? I think it's a lot of hooey, but Shirley MacLaine makes more money than I do. What about alternative medicine? Lots of that information has begun to go up on the Web, but traditional vendors might still find feeding room at the trough. And then there's always sex, drugs (well, anti-drug literature), and rock-and-roll. Let's not get too proud here, friends. It's survival time.

Information Today, **December 1996**

Established market vendors who want to block newbies from cutting into their traditional markets should develop an intercept strategy. They should start scanning the outer edges of their perimeters, checking the locks on back doors and windows, and ordering a squad of archers to the "unscalable" side of the castle walls. Most importantly, they should try to start thinking like a smart newbie.

Information Today, **December 1997**

… when you design information systems that reach every person, remember to make them more than friendly. Make them fun!

Database Searcher, **September 1992**

When customers do not have the time or energy to research value issues, they usually default to the natural instinct of any consumer—distrust of vendors.

Information Today, **October 1994**

[*I worry*] about the possible future information malpractice litigation when current industry practices placing responsibility for most search safety precautions on searchers (pluralization/singularization, rigid field formats, etc.) hit the glowing, naïve expectations of inexperienced end-user searchers. Studies in medical malpractice have shown that lawsuits usually fall not upon the most inept physicians, but upon the ones with the worst bedside manners. While the online industry works on fixing its longstanding quality protection problems, it might do well to learn to smile a lot and ask the searcher where it hurts.

Database Searcher, **July 1989**

And the last rule, when you have a good, effective, usable product—market the hell out of it. Sell it hard. Tout it loudly. Go for broke. In today's world, none but the brave deserve the fair.

Information Today, **March 1996**

Strategy Seven: New Profit Models

Third parties treat content as a promotional device. They would no more consider charging for it than a department store would try to charge people for viewing its window displays. Understanding this reality, Powerize. com has committed itself to delivering to third parties exactly what they want: eyeballs, sticky eyeballs.

Information Today, **October 1999**

One would hope that the designers of the [*Perfect Information Portal*] would devote as much care and consideration in designing advertiser-related presentations as they do designing content. First, of course, they should provide regular, ongoing mechanisms for users to report their general and specific observations on the advertisements they see.

For example, one of these days someone at www. washingtonpost.com is going to ask me about the ads they attach to their crossword puzzle pages. And will they get an earful! For some unimaginable reason, all the ads on that page seem to focus on highly localized events: "Come on down to RFK Stadium this weekend!" or "Buy your belts on the Beltway."

Crossword puzzle addicts from all over the country, if not the world, probably link to this site, one of the few good, free crosswords on the Web. So why don't they advertise things that sell nationally and items of particular appeal to wordsmiths who love crosswords, like books, games, and magazines? Sheesh! Ask people what they want in terms of ads and they may give you some very good advice.

Information Today, **February 2000**

Quint's Laws for Vendors

Rule One: Looking stupid does not constitute a good advertising image for a company in the information business. Text databases that can't spell look stupid, especially in key fields like "United States" in the country field (Our Marketing Slogan: Where-Am-I?). Directory databases that use "The" as a filing point look stupid. Connect-time pricing that rewards the information industry for flawed products by lengthening the time searchers must remain online to find hidden answers does not *look* stupid. However, it *is* stupid since it stifles industry growth by creating the negative impression in customer minds that online vendors prefer valueless revenue to value-driven revenue.

Rule Two: The question defines the answer; the questioner, the success of the answer machine. Design the information service to meet the needs of real questions from real requestors. Rank questions by frequency and type. Identify how different types of searchers ask different types of questions. For the most frequent questions, make sure that your data will meet the searcher's expectations. When it comes to end-users, market the data only when it is ready for their needs. Price for the value of the answer to the customer. If you need more money, get more customers.

Information Today, **March 1993**

Quint's Laws for Vendors on Dealing with the Press

Herewith, some advice on key factors for good relations with the national press:

Availability: Be there when they call. It's not fair and it's not fun, but deadlines drive the presses. Reporters who cannot reach legitimate contacts in time will alter stories to use the best information in hand instead of the best information.

As they say in Hollywood, "How do you want it—good or Wednesday?"...

Accessibility: Let the press talk to the most knowledgeable staff.

Adequacy: Do your homework in developing material for the press. Don't let little flaws trip you up .... Put dates on all press releases. Include addresses, telephone and Fax numbers, e-mail identification, and contact information for all parties listed. For heaven's sake, if you're selling a new product, include the price. Who's kidding whom around here? ... Be quotable. Beg, borrow, or steal quotable ideas, if it does not come naturally ....

Accuracy: Never, never, never lie to the press. Ignorance is acceptable. Stonewalling is acceptable. But lies and half-truths will turn the press into a pack of howling wolves .... Time marches on, but women, elephants, and the Enemies' lists of disinformed reporters never forget.

Attitude: Be nice. Alright, they yanked you out of a world conference to answer some simple-witted questions indicating a complete lack of knowledge of the subject matter about which they intend to write and publish no matter how ignorant they remain. Be nice anyway ....

No matter how onerous dealing with the press becomes, remember that a good report costs less than an advertisement and a bad report can waste the investment in an ad. And as for the general and business press, think of all those lovely, lovely readers. It makes one's circulation go all bubbly, doesn't it?

Information Today, **March 1993**

Quint's Laws for Vendors on Dealing with the Press: Updated for the Net

The ... "A" rules still apply:

Availability: Writers and editors still like to talk to people, but these days everyone expects information industry firms to have a basic presence on the Web, preferably one whose URL they can surmise from the company name (www.thename.com).

Accessibility: Provide e-mail contact points for your key people. Don't make the only contact point an outside public relations firm.

Adequacy: Keep your Web site material comprehensive. Unlike print material, Web site coverage need not limit itself on the basis of postage.

Accuracy: Keep all your Web information current, no dead links, no month-old data, no mismatches between what customers want and what the Web site gives. You may even face liability risks if you don't.

Annoyeth-Not: Sadly, the old complaints remain in force. Please don't call me to find out if I got your press release. I probably did, along with 300 others. Don't call me, I'll call you. Also, include pricing information whenever possible, even if just ballpark information. In the real world, reader interest can vary greatly based on price alone.

[*A final thought*]

The Web has brought one new complaint. The other day I got a short, crisp e-mail message from a public relations representative for a database company. It simply stated: "New Announcement. Product ... Web site http:// ...."

Let me get this straight. You expect me to fire up my browser, which happens to operate separately from my e-mail communication software, and search out your Web site, then find your press release section, and then print/download or take notes while reading this specific product announcement on screen.

You know, it's bad enough when you can't find a gas station that will wash your car windows, but you know life has gotten ugly when the gas station's owner expects you to wash *his* car's windows. I'm glad you've got this information on your Web site, but while you're e-mailing me, just include the press release text! And, by the way, make sure it's text-only. In this virus-ridden world, I don't take encoded documents—even Word.

Information Today, **April 1998**

Chapter 5

SCHOLARLY PUBLISHING

While Barbara wants database vendors to improve and survive, she has no such tender concern for scholarly publishers, who, in her view, have been running a lucrative racket. Their reason for existence—assisting scholarly communication—is endangered by their outrageous subscription prices, jacked up on an annual basis, which have imperiled library book budgets and forced massive subscription cancellations. Worse, the publishers then filed suit to restrict scholars' ability to make photocopies from the journals for which they and their libraries had paid through the teeth. Even before the World Wide Web came along, Barbara recognized that the Internet's greatest potential benefit was allowing free and open dissemination of taxpayer-funded research and scholarly communication. It's quite possible that the plan she outlined, detailed here, was the basis for the National Institutes of Health's E-BioMed Initiative.

Copyright and Fair Use

Let's use a little common sense—before it goes completely out of style. Publishers of the world, libraries serve many users. In fact, they measure their success by the number of users served. In fact, they would not buy a book only one user would use. You know that.

Librarians of the world, you cannot abet rip-offs. Publishers and authors have a right to be paid for their product. When librarians plan to use and reuse a product, they should pay for it. If more people paid for what they use on a computer, maybe more publishers could afford to lower the price and encourage even more usage.

Wilson Library Bulletin, **February 1989**

Can anyone here remember the world before Xerox? A world where reading a journal meant buying a journal or knowing a friendly person or institution that owned it? A world in which only an author could say, "I'll send you a copy," because only the author had a drawerful of reprints? A world where only substantial libraries bought abstract or indexing services because only libraries had the periodical collections to back them up?

Information Today, **October 1992**

In any case, existing [*Copyright Clearance Center*] procedures mean the smaller the firm, the more vast the paperwork. As time and publishers' lawyers march on, companies may find themselves guarding copying machines to prevent "opportunity crime" by impatient, scofflaw users. You've heard of Unsafe Sex? Meet Unsafe Xerox.

Information Today, **October 1992**

[*Re: the Texaco case, in which a court limited the right of corporations to freely copy articles from journals for which its library paid*]

On July 22, 1992, the world ended. You may not have noticed. The mills of the gods grind slow, but they grind exceeding fine. It may take a while—a few months, a few years—before the mills pulverize your part of the planet. Have no hope, though. The world has ended.

Wilson Library Bulletin, **December 1992**

On the other hand, copyright law does not have the same significance as the Bill of Rights, which some publishers seem to think it should. Basically copyright to me is a pragmatic necessity for solving a particular market problem or social need. If creators of intellectual property cannot get paid for their work, they may cease to create, or to create in sufficient quantity.

Wilson Library Bulletin, **January 1994**

User-Hostile Publishers

Let's start with the most forlorn group ... scholarly primary publishers. There they sit with a pile of money, no friends, and no future.

Information Today, **July/August 1995**

Current actions taken by many scholarly publishers— e.g., the Texaco copyright case—are hostile to the interests of librarians, other information professionals, and their clients. Information professionals should fight back using whatever resources or leverage they have in the most effective manner.

Searcher, **February 1995**

Commercial scholarly publishers have an exposed flank, a blind side that stretches from horizon to horizon. They differ from trade or general press. They do not pay for the creation of the product they sell.

Commercial scholarly publishers do not pay authors. They even have the nerve to charge authors for providing them material they sell. They do not—or barely—pay editors. They do not pay peer reviewers. They do not contribute to the funding of research. They do not contribute to the creation of new researchers through scholarships or other educational programs.

If the authors and/or editors walked out on them and started delivering their scholarly contributions through other routes, there would not be a damn thing the commercial scholarly publishers could do about it. And with the Internet out there linking scholarly communication into an electronic publishing medium, the laser printing is on the wall.

Information Today, **June 1995**

Of course scholarly publishers might show wisdom, restraint, and even generosity in administering the rights that the courts [*in the Texaco case*] may have given them.

They may rise above venal considerations of immediate profit and consider the potential damage to scholarship .... Why, you're right! That's not the sky falling! It's a pork chop dropping off a flying pig!

These are the same scholarly publishers who have whipsawed library budgets for decades with launch after launch of more and more minusculely focused journals. These are the same ones who have maintained double-digit inflation rates year after year. These are the same scholarly publishers who never pay a red cent to any author or almost any editor for contributions, who even have the crust to bill authors page charges for giving them the material they sell ....

Wilson Library Bulletin, **December 1992**

If someone's going to get rich from scholarly publishing, shouldn't it be the scholars or the people who pay the scholars' salaries?

Searcher, **September 1999**

Libraries have shrinking budgets and commercial scholarly publishers have unshrinking expectations.

Information Today, **June 1995**

Commercial scholarly publishers seem to have set a course deliberately designed to destroy markets, attack allies, and eliminate essential assets. The only discernable benefits of the strategy would seem to lie in very-short-term revenue extraction, but the cost of the quick cash would seem to be their future existence.

Information Today, June 1995

… the resentment of having to pay for something you already own keeps recurring in discussions with users of legal information.

Information Today, April 1996

[*Article header: "Saw Ally; Shot Same"*]

Why on earth would commercial scholarly publishers want to risk reducing coverage of their material in indexing and abstracting services? It would be like a book publisher trying to charge the *New York Times* for review copies. For the few bucks it takes to mail extra copies of a journal, publishers get their material indexed and advertised to untold numbers of users. And they don't even have to pay for the service.

Information Today, June 1995

Recent developments seem to confirm that commercial scholarly publishers have fallen into the grip of some primal self-destructive urge and—lemming-like—have chosen to take their summer vacation at the shore, a bourne from which no lemming returneth.

Perhaps technology has its own mythological way of notifying subspecies that their time is up. Perhaps the Internet, that terrifyingly inchoate force of the New World Order, has sent some silent, socio-biological signal, and commercial scholarly print publishers have responded by rising and exiting the world stage in mute acceptance of their doom.

Information Today, **June 1995**

Solution One: Cut Publishers Out

To substitute for existing scholarly channels, the Internet needs an archiving function to guarantee availability and delivery of a definitive, author-approved version of a piece of scholarship.

It needs specific peer review mechanisms that refine the communication threads that, if archived after evaluation, could better the peer review system now in use with traditional publications.

It needs access tools for the archived material, abstracting and indexing of the ocean tides of data flowing over the system.

And last, it needs doers to perform the above tasks. The offer is open in that area. Scholarly publishers ... still may consider the net the enemy. On the other hand, abstracting and indexing services could see an opportunity to expand exponentially if they could conquer the new environment. Search services might even take a whack at it. For that matter, why shouldn't librarians join the race?

Wilson Library Bulletin, **December 1992**

[*That's no misprint. This was written in 1992, when the Internet was still inhabited by gophers.*]

The [*National Institutes of Health*] and Public Health Service fund a substantial portion of the world's top medical research. The NIH has a standing rule in its grants stipulating that the NIH cannot be charged for the reproduction of research produced by its funds and used for achieving its ends.

At present, NIH legal staff apply this rule to cover intramural participants in intramural research. However, NIH counsel indicates there is no reason why the rule could not extend to more general application, e.g., to all researchers working under NIH grants or even to all medical researchers that might somehow contribute to the nation's health. Like all federal agencies, the NIH needs to conserve its resources. At present, it supports publication of NIH-funded medical research in peer-reviewed scholarly journals and relies on those journals for dissemination of scholarship.

The [*National Library of Medicine*], in conjunction with other interested parties such as the Medical Library Association (MLA) should undertake a joint project to produce a sound working system for stabilized Internet research dissemination. The system should solve all major problems in archiving, filtering, and access that still inhibit Internet dominance. The mode developed should have enough flexibility to apply to other areas of scholarship outside medical research.

The NLM and participating medical libraries would maintain archives and supply print and alternative media output from NIH-certified NIRs to all interested users. Such support would include current awareness services covering both print sources and electronic services. Electronic services would include optional membership sign-ups for key listservs or newsgroups. Participating libraries would offer to deliver electronic "articles" with graphics, pictures, tables, etc., through commitment to certain national and international technical standards.

When complete, the NLM should propose that NIH stipulate in its grants that publication support funds will be available only for the new electronic publishing.

Searcher, **February 1995**

[*In September 1999, the National Institutes of Health announced their E-BioMed Initiative, which bears a remarkable resemblance to what Barbara outlined here.*]

This scenario was only one of many possibilities. Think hard. Examine your resources. Check your networks and connections. Look to your clients for leverage. Identify the interests of each party you can reach in the issue of control and dissemination of research.

Some areas that might prove fruitful:

1. University Research Presses.

University research presses could serve as central clearinghouses for contributing faculty material to electronic archives. They could get the credit and identification of the university as the source of the research ....

2. Scholarly Societies.

Sadly, many scholarly societies imitate the most profit-oriented publishers .... Nevertheless, a scholarly society's membership usually incorporates the authors and readers of research in that field. Members educated to see the advantage of generous dissemination as the primary proper goal of scholarly publishing could mandate such policy goals ....

3. Author's Retention of Control.

Authors of scholarly research should retain control of their own copyright beyond initial publication.

Searcher, **February 1995**

Back in February 1995, I wrote an editorial in *Searcher* called "Battle Plan" that outlined three major approaches for restructuring—with fire and sword if necessary—the user-hostile world of scholarly publishing.

… The approach that I recommended as having the best chance of success seems to have finally begun. Hallelujah! And I don't give a snap of my fingers if no one connected with the current effort ever read my prescient words of wisdom. (Insert halo here.) I just want the idea to become reality, and fast.

Information Today, **September 1999**

The E-BioMed concept is designed to exploit every advantage offered by electronic publishing: quick delivery; fast processing; single search engine access; full image and multimedia; cheap archiving; open peer review; hyperlinking to relevant related material; customized personal journals; e-mail announcements and distribution of browsable tables of contents; direct interactivity with authors, reviewers, and readers; etc.

It will also allow for full-length presentations of life science studies that include all the supporting documentation, details on methods, and even large data sets that print length restrictions often cut out.

Best of all, the E-BioMed concept plans to deliver all this material to the world public in perpetuity for free! Ain't that grand?

Information Today, **September 1999**

As one might surmise, the oxen whom the success of this new initiative would gore have already begun bellowing. (Why wait till you actually feel the puncture and loss of blood starts to weaken your yowls? Roar and stagger about dramatically while you still have your strength. These are medical experts, after all.)

Information Today, **September 1999**

Solution Two: How Scholarly Publishers Might Survive

First: Try Not To Lose.

In which direction should scholarly publishers turn? So far, they seem to have looked primarily to the distribution function, focusing on the reader. This puts their horse-and-buggy approach to technology onto the fast lane of the superhighway. Not a good idea. The distribution side of the field is where all the action and hype circulate, but it is also where all the big-time competition is already shoving and pushing for Lebensraum.

Second: Try To Win.

… Instead, publishers should look to the area that lacks resources, where their investments can make a real impact, where each dollar counts double. In other words, publishers should look to the other side of the bridge, to the creation of research. It's the research arena where funding shrinks daily.

... It's important for publishers who turn to research support to change their attitudes. They should not think of the move as primarily a defensive strategy designed to maintain control of a publishable product. Instead they should embrace the research opportunities fully. They have the opportunity to get the inside track on tomorrow's technologies and services, to find the hot-shot infrapreneurs and entrepreneurs whose future companies will appear on NASDAQ commercials in 2007, and to get royalties and shares of patent rights. The publisher investors could also link faculty into distance learning networks that serve other corporate and government investors and funders. Publishers that "own" the research by investing in its creation could also someday return to the distribution side with a lot stronger position than they have today.

Information Today, July/August 1995

Publisher-investors could fill some of the shoes that government research funding agencies have left empty ....

How could the "house percentage" factor work for publisher-investors? Well, publishers might want to ensure intellectual property conditions across the board in research facilities and universities. Once they have research structured enough to ensure payment, they could take their percentage like a Hollywood agent. Following that insidious defensive strategy that keeps creeping into the game, they could extend intellectual property coverage through an archive facility for the new distribution medium. People love to think their ideas are unique and marketable. Publishers could offer to protect the property of people all over the Internet who want to archive their material, like the deposit function in ATM machines. As more and more researchers turn into consultants and interpreters of scholarship, publishers could facilitate multimedia delivery of product and expand networks of clients and contacts. Again, for a percentage.

... Putting money into the research process could gain publishers a real property right in future technology and services. It could also salvage their tattered reputation for service to the research community, reverting them back into friends and partners with the people who make it happen. The research and education community will remember who stands by them in the current crisis. Now is the time for all smart publishers to rise to the opportunity.

Information Today, July/August 1995

Chapter 6

RANDOM MUSINGS

Censorship

Basically most people want to engineer silences as well as sounds.

Information Today, January 1996

Censorship is an itch of long standing, an itch that crawled out of the caves with the human animal, an itch that won't go away. Considered on its broadest level, maybe it shouldn't go away.

Review your own lives, especially those of you over a certain age (and any age is a certain age). Don't you find yourself almost as appreciative of some of the things you have never known, never heard, never thought of as you are of the things that you have? How many of us shake our heads and tsk-tsk at the deplorable depravities of the "other generation?"

Of course, what each person considers depravity varies. For some, it may mean ladies without hats and gloves on a public street; for others, it means ladies of the street. Some may condemn rap music ("Albums to Commit Felonies By"), others, New Age sound ("Will somebody puh-leez shut that elevator door?!").

Information Today, January 1996

Hurricanes of data can lead even the chronically curious to shut the door on an open mind—at least until the winds die down.

Information Today, January 1996

After all, the price of affluence is a confusion of choices.

Searcher, July/August 1998

And so people turn to censorship, to systems that shut off information flow. The more massive the data flow and the more stress factors related to the data content, the more the censorship reaction occurs. Can we stop it? No. Should we try to stop it? Maybe not.

Information Today, January 1996

The dark side of censorship usually occurs when people try to control not just what they themselves experience, but what others can experience as well. Although people may have a right to not listen, to not research, to not have to argue their positions, they don't necessarily have the right to force on others the same silence or to deny others the information needed to satisfy personal goals and beliefs.

Information Today, January 1996

Borderline areas occur when one person does have legitimate responsibility for the minds of others, such as parents for children or teachers for pupils. As a rule, the closer the monitor and the monitored come to a peer relationship, the less the legitimacy of the control. So parents of two-year-olds have more right to control the perceived reality of their progeny than parents of 12-year-olds, and practically none over 22-year-olds. Kindergarten teachers have more sway than college professors.

Information Today, **January 1996**

People oppose censorship because they do not want truth silenced, but people support censorship because they do not want truth buried under a deluge of lies, half-truths, and noise. Even ardent defenders of academic freedom, for example, will often still endure the "censorship" of the peer review standards of scholarship.

Information Today, **January 1996**

Democracy, Government, and Citizens

What is government for anyway? Isn't it supposed to help its constituents, to contribute to the economy, to maximize the value of the dollars given it by taxpayers? If all government agencies had to recover their costs, someone would have shut down Amtrak and the Postal Service years ago. I'm not opposed to fiscal sanity or solvency, but one has to look at the bigger picture. Sometimes you have to spend money to make money. Sometimes you have to look at the larger economy to find out whether an expenditure was worth the investment.

Searcher, **October 1999**

Citizens are a greedy bunch .... And why not? After all, it's our country, our government, our tax dollars. Probably the most revolutionary concept behind the American Revolution was the theory that governments exist to serve the people, not the other way around, and that only the people can determine whether they are well served.

Information Today, **April 1996**

The [*mass e-mailing of racist messages*] served as just another reminder of how eggshell fragile, how humming-bird-delicate are the civilities that form the basis of Internet communities. In fact, it reminds us of the vulner-ability ingrained in the very concept of democracy. Still, how fragile is an eggshell? Step outside of a morning and hear the birds singing. They are living proof of the egg's superior design and the shell's durability. Eggs are even sat upon. And how delicate is a hummingbird? If you could eat twice your weight in a day and still flap your arms faster than the human eye can see, you'd make the cover of a Superhero comic book.

Searcher, **November/December 1994**

Maybe democracy isn't as vulnerable as it looks. Maybe just letting people do whatever they decide to do isn't as crazy as it sounds. Maybe the concept of democracy is built on every parent's realization of the nightmare truth that, in the end, the only way to prove [*people*] trustworthy is to trust them.

Searcher, **November/December 1994**

I've always thought that the great underlying stability of the American experiment was symbolized in the fact that U.S. spells "us." No matter how miffed or murderous one grows toward government policies, one always has these midnight reality checks. Whose fault was it anyway? What if … I'd voted in the last election? What if … I'd gotten involved before the primaries? What if … I didn't slam the door on that guy with the petition?

Searcher, **November/December 1994**

Of course … all governments, like all economic institutions, require feedback from—you guessed it—people. Whether or not you listen and act on the advice, any smart government, like any smart marketer, will offer people at least the illusion that they have a voice in their fate, that someone's listening. The safety valve factor alone makes such procedures essential. The lack of feedback, more than any other factor in my opinion, finally defeated communism.

Searcher, **November/December 1994**

The direct research funding tends to support the general growth of a better world with a bigger economy and better technologies. From such a world come happier taxpayers and more contented constituents, or such is the government's assumption. And with research serving its own operations, the government has grown big and efficient—well, at least big.

Maybe the citizens aren't crazy about the size of the government, but if you applied a corporation's standard of success, growing in scope and size and performance would constitute a victory.

Information Today, **July/August 1995**

They don't call courts "courts" for nothing. The divine right of kings dies hard.

Information Today, **April 1996**

Danger to the Information Infrastructure

Even technological drunkards such as myself find the times sobering. For years, we have wallowed in the wealth of information pouring through our machines and perhaps even considered ourselves impervious to the nickel-and-dime, mundane concerns of traditional information channels ....

And frankly, I'm thinking that maybe a strong support of traditional information sources, familiar information channels, even (dare I say it?) the print medium may be in order. Now is the time for all good information professionals to come to the aid of the information infrastructure.

Database Searcher, **October 1992**

Well, the high-rolling '80s are over and the recovery '90s are upon us. The basic foundations of many information services are at risk. And no matter what any fast-talking, gold-chained, blow-dried architect/engineer tells you—if the foundation goes, so does the penthouse ....

Let's start with the lowest damage levels. Without healthy libraries, where will buyers get the wide variety of documents discovered in bibliographic searches? Without the right to reproduce articles (imperiled by the Texaco copyright case), why do a literature search in the first place?

But the damage spreads. Without healthy government statistical agencies, who produces the raw numbers that drive the fancy financial and econometric databases? Without healthy government research funding, who produces the scientific and technical research that fills the reports? Without healthy support for higher education programs, who produces the scholars that produce the research? Without healthy support for general education, who produces the readers or citizens willing to vote for public research funding?

Database Searcher, October 1992

[*Re: the Tasini case that ruled database publishers cannot use authors' work without reimbursing them*]

I've decided I would like the Tasini decision to go away, at least the decision as left by the last appeals court. Well, maybe not go away completely. After all, I'm a freelance writer myself. But the pennies authors could get for online use don't justify the disastrous burden that counting those pennies and mailing them to authors would create for publishers, aggregators, search services, and even professional searchers. It would be like mailing in a claim for a 10-cent rebate—the stamp costs 33 cents.

Worse than the actual dollars involved, the removing of items not covered would dismantle the existing full-text structures and completely inhibit attempts to further expand the body of published material available off-line. Already we hear stories from major aggregators about publishers withdrawing content that's been available for years or, at least, about rescinding permission for new spin-off products.

Information Today, November 2000

And look at the latest hot trend in software delivery—Application Service Providers (ASPs). This development assumes that masses of users will accept something that one would not have thought anyone would even consider just a few years ago—namely, that one should let outsiders know every time you use their software, even let outsiders handle all the data you produce. This trend certainly appears to run counter to the increasing public concern with Internet privacy, but all the gurus claim it's the coming thing.

Personally, I draw the line in the sand. I'm no privacy nut, but if Bill Gates thinks he's going to know every time one of my fingers hits the keyboard, much less which key it hits, he's got another think coming. Didn't many of us flee to the personal computer in the first place in an attempt to escape the tyranny of centralized computing services in our institutions? So now, everyone wants to convert their desktop computer environment into a nouveau MIS-controlled installation? I don't think so.

Searcher, October 2000

On Editing

Tracking talent is never useless. As a missionary, I always like to keep my network of visionaries current. You would be surprised how often you find the same visionaries and missionaries behind new product developments—even at different firms. It takes a little longer to make a dream a reality than to maintain a reality, but it does get done sometimes.

Information Today, **December 1992**

[*On courting writers*]
Someday, I should calculate how many hours per article I spend lurking in tree tops, waiting to pounce on unsuspecting talent.

Searcher, **May 2000**

Should I write a column on a topic that I do not fully understand myself? Maybe my readers need whatever information I have, even if it is not perfect. But then again, perhaps my readers will demand more than I have to give. If those readers of mine can't cut me some slack after all these years, to heck with them!

Wilson Library Bulletin, **March 1992**

Every editor loves to hear from readers. For one thing, it confirms the fact that the readers really exist, that someone out there actually listens, that one has not chosen a profession that leaves one all alone, talking to oneself.

Searcher, **November/December 1999**

As you may have guessed by now, my editorial policy remains to tell the truth, the whole truth, and nothing but the truth. It's fairer to all parties.

Information Today, **May 1993**

On Trade Publications

When are the reporters and editors of general and business press going to learn the basic history of the wide world of databases? Are they ever going to do some research before they pass off uneducated guesswork as reality in their writings? Could they at least promise to turn over a new leaf research-wise when it comes to the database history of their own publications?

… In case the journalists of the world haven't heard, there was online before the Web.

Information Today, April 1997

When you see articles or coverage that ignores your existence, follow up quickly. There are people who read the letters to the editor sections first and foremost in any magazine. As the beloved publisher of both this newspaper and my own publication has said many times, "Heat sells better than light." People like to see fur fly. They like to watch experts dispute their expertise. They enjoy watching someone tell established authorities that they've goofed.

Information Today, April 1997

Technology and Its Effects

Most important of all, at the end of the 19th century, people around the world had come to expect technological change, to assume that it would occur, to believe that tomorrow would

not look like today. That expectation produced an acceptance—grudging or hopeful—that in turn drove more
change, if only by eliciting capital investment for high-
tech developments.

Searcher, **November/December 1999**

More than anything else, the key societal change that led
to the acceleration of technological change was the belief in
the ordinariness of invention.

Searcher, **May 1996**

The common reference points of Western civilization were
challenged and, in many cases, overturned. Some may simply have gone underground to rise again. After the rise of the
telephone, intelligentsia mourned the death of writing as a
general skill, but e-mail seems to have brought it back.

... The demise of a common religion, not to mention a
classical education, has challenged the ability to create a
common public ethic, but tolerance has emerged as a dominant public ethics standard.

Searcher, **November/December 1999**

The price tag for political action and leadership has
dropped. The price for centralized repression of information
has risen. In China, aged leaders have tried to impose lip
service to their reconstruction of the Tiannenmen massacre
and subsequent repressions on all foreign contacts. They only
succeeded in making themselves look as senile as their politics.

Wilson Library Bulletin, **September 1989**

Still the best comment on CNN's strutting [*during the Gulf War*] may have been Johnny Carson's request for the phone number of Saddam Hussein's cable service. As Johnny pointed out, "In Malibu, HBO goes out when it rains. Hussein is under aerial bombardment and still gets cable?"

Canadian Journal of Information Science, **April 1992**

One thing Desert Storm, first war of the New World Order, bore out: the new Latin is English. C-SPAN, the cable network carrying unedited no-commentary news events, regularly showed press conferences conducted by each major ally in the war. All were conducted in English.

Canadian Journal of Information Science, **April 1992**

What brought the Communist Empire to collapse? Another dissertation for another day. But this writer would suggest: a lack of feedback. You can't do anything right, or even learn how much trouble you're in, if you don't listen.

Searcher, **October 1998**

Of course, there's no such thing as a free lunch (except in perceptions of Web costs), and the revolution has a downside. It may be that none of those who started it will survive it. Sort of like the French Revolution. Once they got the guillotine lubed, they kind of liked to keep it humming along. So when they ran out of "aristos" to execute, they moved on to passé revolutionaries.

Information Today, **September 1997**

All cutting-edge technologies can cut two ways. One reality that will distinguish the next millennium is the loss of forgetting. Imagine living in a world that cannot forget, that remembers and stores everything—every image, every word, every document, every joke, every insult, every message, every call. Are you cringing?

Searcher, January 2000

Once people have developed the habit of relying on computers as memory substitutes, they will never turn back.

Searcher, January 2000

With full Internet and Web connections, people could pick their virtual realities. Vendors won't mind as long as they can make a sale. In late 1999, *The Wall Street Journal* ran an article on Microsoft's Encarta encyclopaedia which revealed that Microsoft offered different facts for different cultures. For example, an under-appreciated Italian-American invented the telephone in the Italian language edition, while Alexander Graham Bell continued to prevail in English-language and German editions. Will non-virtual societies begin to disintegrate as individuals select their realities, define their peers, and commit to new loyalties?

Searcher, January 2000

[*Apropos: the discovery of the flawed Pentium chip and the subsequent Intel market drop*]

If you thought shooting at the White House had become a popular new sport, stock manipulation via Internet messages may vie for Olympic Games status.

Wilson Library Bulletin, March, 1995

[Written five years before a teenager made a fortune in stocks he talked up in chat rooms]

As we segued smoothly back to the [*O. J. Simpson*] trial, I got the curious sensation that reality may have begun to structure itself around the time and resource specifications of television production schedules.

How disciplined and economical reality has become. A question arises in an ongoing news event, news media report the concern, reliable sources hear the report and contact investigative reporters and analysts, and the matter is settled in the 15-minute time slot available, minus time for commercials.

Talk about nature imitating art! One has to pity the sequestered jurors who can only listen to court-censored testimony. If only they knew!

Information Today, April 1995

Have you ever thought how much good you could have done for your inner self if you had assigned the memory cells in your brain to remember the words of Shakespeare, or even arcane provisions of the Internal Revenue Code, instead of dedicating them to the words of Speedy Alka-Seltzer or whether "Mikey" would eat his cereal?

Searcher, April 1997

[On seeing a program about the discovery of a tool used for centuries to weave fishing nets]

I confess a cold chill went down my spine at the idea of a culture that had not changed its line of work for 15 centuries. Some longstanding traditions—bread recipes, sleeve shapes, foot races, etc.—are just fine. But a people that could get up each morning and trot off to work with this little doohickey in their pocket for a millennium and a half (and counting) without ever considering the options of getting into another line of work or substantially improving the technology or just blowing town—wow, that's just a little more inertia than I like to see in humans. We all have slow days, but 1,500 years—whoof.

Searcher, **May 1996**

Y2K

… one does wonder on what grounds the U.S. Congress could justify an anticipatory bail-out bill for litigation stemming from Y2K problems ("Honestly, judge, it isn't fair. How could anyone expect Ph.D. engineers to know some other number came after 1,999?!").

Searcher, **January 2000**

I have always suspected that Y2K difficulties did not derive just from the pressure that 80-digit keypunch cards put on programmers to shorten date references in the early days of computers. The 2-digit field assigned to years may also have stemmed from a 1950s, 1960s, 1970s unspoken assumption that mankind would never reach the next millennium—or not with its computer paraphernalia intact, in any event.

Searcher, **November/December 1999**

Taking Risks

Many years ago, I learned (oddly enough at a management training seminar) that in the real world, the definition of success doesn't just mean winning. It also extends to losing acceptably, i.e., losing in a crowd.

… We've all heard the old line, "No one ever got fired for buying IBM." It means that people don't necessarily lose their jobs for making a mistake; they get the axe for making showy, original, daring, and—in particular—lonely mistakes. As long as you commit an error that hundreds or thousands of others have committed, you're probably OK.

Information Today, **December 1997**

And one last tip for information managers. How long is it since you considered or suggested a policy change … that made you sweat or scared the hell out of you? If it has been more than a year, you're not doing your job.

Canadian Journal of Information Science, **April 1992**

The Biggest Risk: Going It Alone

So you've decided—with or without the assistance of the depression or other negative external factors—to market your library skills door to door. Welcome to the wild blue yonder. How does it feel to float through the air with the wind in your hair? By the way, did you remember to pack a parachute?

Wilson Library Bulletin, **May 1992**

As a group, information brokers worry a lot. On the other hand, they're a group with nerve as well as nerves. Each job completed, each satisfied client, each year in business, each business plan goal attained makes them stronger and more confident.

God help you if you join them, for independence can become addictive. In time you'll find it hard to envision living "under the yoke" of a bureaucratic chain of command. Don't worry too much about it. The federal government has set up a very effective addiction rehabilitation program. If you need to sober up, just contact the IRS. Or wait, and they'll get a hold of you.

Wilson Library Bulletin, **May 1992**

On Truth

Only people who respect each other enough to tell the truth, as each sees it, can change one another's thinking. Quarreling ruins good arguments.

Information Today, **November 1996**

Tell a lie often enough and it comes to smell true. Make the lie big enough and the sheer size will induce belief. After all, where there's smoke, there's fire. Where there's a forest fire, there must be a forest.

Information Today, **April 1993**

… it's never safe not to recognize danger or opportunity. If you don't speak the truth, in time you'll stop looking for it, and then stop finding it. And in time, truth will find you when you're not looking.

And anyway, truth is a lot more fun.

Searcher, **June 1995**

You'd be surprised how rare a quality telling the truth is. Or would you?

Searcher, **June 1995**

Why do I have such a strong impression of [*Myra Grenier*] as a formative figure in my professional life? Because she was the first "boss," the first member of the elite manager class, that I ever met who always told the truth. That means two things. She saw the truth and she spoke the truth. She cared about information service, information technology, her clients. From that care came concentrated attention to developments in the field and the questions behind the questions. When she saw what would work, she called it as she saw it. She espoused the best publicly and openly. When something didn't work, she pointed out the failure as the first step in the endeavor to change it.

Searcher, **June 1995**

On Management

Do smart managements know the value of good information service? Of course, but we all know stories of even smart management doing dumb things. And who says all our managements are smart? ... Or maybe the smart management just has a different agenda—like sacrificing some of the long-range strength of an institution to the short-range goal of downsizing and cost reduction. And then, of course, a too-smart manager may have just answered the age-old question in the age-old manner, "It was either you or me and it just boiled down to you."

Searcher, **November/December 1996**

[On being forced to take part in a team-building survival exercise]

Basically the winning wisdom that evolved from the group disagreed with mine (pause for shocked gasps!). The policy they settled upon would not have achieved the grand goals for the institution promised by the new technologies under discussion, but it would have maintained the continued employment and job tenure of the group's members. I thought the group would go for the gold, reach for the stars, but instead they chose a policy that would fail but fail acceptably—complementing their professional acumen and virtuous intentions while blaming their failure on limited resources. Just a nice survival strategy by bureaucratic realists.

Searcher, **September 1999**

On Learning and Memory

They say that one of the great gifts of human design is the inability to remember pain. Unfortunately, the downside of that gift is a certain flattening of the learning curve.

Wilson Library Bulletin, January 1993

Fun tasks are very important if you expect people to spend substantial personal time on a learning task.

Searcher, May 1995

The fact of the matter is that once again knowledge will piggyback on pleasure's shoulders. If information professionals want to measure the advance of information technology into mass markets, look to leisure and entertainment products before you look to decision aids and databases. It's the world of leisure that supplies cheap compact disc players that ushered in CD-ROM databases.

Database Searcher, September 1992

History teaches many lessons. Unfortunately sometimes the good students are dyslexic and seated in the back of the classroom; the bad students spend all their time disrupting discussions; and the indifferent majority yawn and slip into slumber. Worst of all, however, the teacher—named Clio, according to the ancient Greeks—has lost both the curriculum and the lesson plans .…

Searcher, April 2000

What is it about the psychology of errors? Why is it so threatening? Simple ignorance works differently. When you realize you need to know something about which you have no or insufficient knowledge, you treat that as a problem and apply standard problem solving approaches. What exactly do I need to know? What would be the advantages of acquiring this information? What would be the consequences of continued ignorance in this matter? Where could I find this information? With what degree of completeness? For what expenditure of resources?

But intrude the specter of error onto the scene and watch the logical approach begin to teeter. Let the ignorant person question whether they should already have known the unknown data and the problems of acquiring new information recede into the background while the psychological state of the unknower comes to the fore.

Instead of using objective judgments, learning decisions become contaminated by ego defense mechanisms. Self-doubt deflects focus from the particular information under discussion. ("Why don't I ever stay on top of things? What else don't I know that I need to know?") Self-justification misestimates the difficulty of acquiring data. ("I can't know everything. Finding out about this kind of thing probably takes too much time and money.") Denial stops the process completely. ("It doesn't matter anyway. I don't really need to know all this stuff.")

Database Searcher, **October 1989**

What is the most precious resource in this Information Age? The human attention span. What is the second most precious resource? The human memory. Sad to say, skimpy as they already are, both resources seem to diminish the more we need them to grow.

Information Today, April 1999

Santayana once wrote that "Those who cannot remember the past are condemned to repeat it." The inference appears to be that the Fates keep scattering banana peels for the human race to slide upon and, unless the species can remember the shape and smell, it will forever find itself a second banana. Memory serves to remind humans of mistakes once made. Memory and creativity provide a vision of how to avoid similar mistakes in the future.

Database Searcher, January 1990

On Improving with Age

I remember as a youth listening with eyebrows hoisted to adult inanities over the unremittingly wonderful times I was supposed to be having. And I resolved then never to forget, to keep a personal time capsule of recorded memory, that youth was also a royal pain .... If asked to define idiocy in terms of personal experience, which of us would not turn instantly to those volumes of our diaries entitled *My Teen Years*?

Wilson Library Bulletin, March 1990

I suspect that youth, particularly adolescence, only maintains its over-hyped image by virtue of memory's deterioration with age.

Wilson Library Bulletin, March 1990

Somewhere long ago I read that as you get older, your ability to learn new facts, to acquire new motor skills, erodes, but your ability to make connections, to synthesize observations into truths, increases. Sometimes, alas, acquiring wisdom can have its down side.

Searcher, **March 2000**

Life can prove an uphill struggle at times, particularly when you embark on a course of self-improvement. [*You end*] up looking back with a tear in [*your*] eye, reminiscing on halcyon days of smug content, before you learned how much had gone wrong with you, how far the distance lay between your current performance and your goal. Change, even for the better, is always so much more pleasant to watch than to experience.

Searcher, **April 1997**

Here's a test of your remaining short-term memory. How old were you when you first figured out that 95 cents at the end of a price tag meant you should add a dollar to the front number and ignore the decimal? Could it be about the same time you discovered "New and Improved" meant "same old, same old?" I used to feel insulted at the lack of respect these ancient old marketing wheezes showed for consumer acumen. Now I feel almost nostalgic.

Information Today, **March 1996**

On Books

The other day I dipped into my storehouse and pulled out a huge tome—one of those classics you always fear becomes a book you "should" read, instead of one you want to read.

Searcher, **July/August 1999**

By the way, if anyone thinks that books are dead, think again. If anyone thinks that the traditional library function of supplying books to patrons is dead, read Steve Coffman's article in [*the July/August issue of* Searcher] re-capping just some of the hundreds of responses he got to his March 1999 cover story on "Building Earth's Largest Library."

Searcher, **July/August 1999**

Personally, I am not an enemy of print (no matter what you hear). Print has strong advantages for specific needs. It is mobile. It stands the belly test. You can lie flat on your stomach or roll over on your back and still read it.

Canadian Journal of Information Science, **April 1992**

Books make questions—a very important function in an age of answers.

Canadian Journal of Information Science, **April 1992**

With print, you can take a client with a vague interest and broaden and deepen that interest until you get a client with real questions, looking for answers instead of background.

Canadian Journal of Information Science, **April 1992**

On Movies

"Well, Stanley, this is another fine mess you've gotten me into." How the poetry of the ancient ones echoes through modern life!

Wilson Library Bulletin, **February 1989**

Any cinéaste will tell you that sometimes the best lines come from the worst movies—well, not the worst, but the flawed .... One of my personal favorites comes from *Dark Passage*, a Bogart-Bacall flick (and if you don't know who they are, kill yourself, it's the only way out with honor).

Searcher, **November/December 1995**

People often develop a kind of natural modesty when it comes to the things they know, particularly knowledge of long standing ("If I know it, anyone can"). A seemly modesty is always pleasant. On the other hand, like most inaccuracies—and think of how long it took you to learn all the things you know—it has a down side. It can also lead to unjust condemnation of those who don't know what you know ("If I know it, everyone should").

Personally, the event that caused this reality to come into focus for me came when a teenage daughter of a friend of mine did not know who Jimmy Stewart was. I couldn't believe any cinematically literate person wouldn't know the star of *It's a Wonderful Life*, not to mention many other of his many films. On the other hand, Stewart had stopped making movies before she was born; in fact, he had stopped starring in movies before I was a teenager. And the golden age of television rerunning black-and-white movies—the era that had induced my cine-mania—had ended long, long ago.

Searcher, **April 2000**

On California

Passenger rail transportation exists in California, but mainly it's just one of those things San Franciscans do when they want to feel "citified." They have a new rail service here in L.A. called the "Blue Line." Unfortunately, they should probably rename it the "Crimson Line" because it keeps making the evening news with tales of blood and gore.

Apparently, citizens of this region—motorists by nature—do not comprehend the physics of railroads. They keep driving or walking on the tracks with tragic consequences that would not shock Easterners but still seem to surprise Californians ("But if it can't stop, why do they let it go so fast? And you say it can't swerve, either?").

Information Today, **February 1996**

Unless you are reading this article somewhere in Southern California, you may well ask, "What does all this mean to me? I've already paid the portion of my taxes that goes to the Annual California Disaster Fund from FEMA [*Federal Emergency Management Agency*]. I believe it was floods this year. Next year, locusts, no doubt. Frankly, California's propensity for Cinemascope, 'Film at Eleven' disasters is getting a little old. I notice that their expensive troubles and woes never prevent the Rose Parade from shoving their sunny climate in our frostbitten faces each New Year's Day."

Information Today, **February 1995**

This and That

Shouldn't the Environmental Protection Agency or the Occupational Safety and Health Administration be informed that business travelers constitute abused workers? Have regulatory agencies in the nation's capital so far forgotten their responsibilities as to allow whole classes of employees to be strapped into a cramped space for hours on end, only to be flung on wobbly knees while loaded down with misshapen lumps of heavy luggage for mile-long walks down slippery-footed corridors to whatever climate awaits them when the last door springs open?

Wilson Library Bulletin, January 1993

Or what about spam? We all hate it, but it's hard to avoid and still experience the full serendipity of the Net. How do you filter it creatively? What about a "ping" test? I've noticed that if you hit the Reply button and tell a spammer to go away, the message almost always gets returned as undeliverable. Notice the spammers don't like getting what they give.

I'd pay extra to an Internet service provider who ran through my incoming e-mail and tested to see when the Reply function wouldn't work. They could then shove all messages from people who didn't want a response into a separate folder for me to peruse at my leisure—or trash in one fell swoop. See? More information drives a solution to bad information.

Searcher, July/August 2000

Chapter 7

WORDS TO LIVE BY

You can't expect a life without problems, but if you work hard and smart, you at least get a respectable class of problems, problems you can be proud of.

Information Today, **November 1993**

The trouble with miracles is figuring out the installation instructions.

Wilson Library Bulletin, **December 1994**

So what giant steps can we take to make a Golden Age from the days that lie before us? Well, frankly, it's those giant steps that usually lead to tripping and falling; shorter, surer steps—but in the right direction—can cover more distance.

Searcher, **February 2000**

When all is said and done, the only irreplaceable resource in the world is Time.

Searcher, **February 2000**

After all, even though there may be no such thing as a free lunch, if someone else picks up the tab, that's close enough for most people.

Information Today, **April 1998**

But inaccuracies can occur on both the upside and the downside of self-esteem. Sometimes the gift of seeing ourselves as others see us can compliment, can decry false modesty, can challenge us to live up to our full potential.

Searcher, **February 1999**

… ignorance often succeeds by being satisfied with partial victories.

Information Today, **April 1999**

The trouble with moral precepts is that they're always a lot easier to pronounce than to perform. The phrases may fall trippingly off the tongue, but the real tripping occurs when you try to walk the walk, not just talk the talk.

Searcher, **June 2000**

If online is the answer, what is the question?

SCOUG motto

Without a keen appreciation of irony, could any of us make it through human existence?

Database Searcher, **September 1992**

"The Loneliness of Logic."

Title of one of Barbara's articles in *Searcher*, **June 1995**

Actually, yesterdays can be the greatest enemies. They lure one into thinking that today is a little less real and tomorrow a lot further off.

Searcher, **November/December 1995**

Even personal experience teaches a short memory can be a prerequisite for friendship.

Database Searcher, **January 1990**

You know the old saying, "When something sounds too good to be true, it probably is." Well, there's a corollary to that wise old adage. "When something doesn't sound at all, someone probably doesn't want you to know about it."

Information Today, **May 1993**

P. T. Barnum was of the opinion that there is no such thing as bad publicity, but then he ran a freak show.

Information Today, **September 1995**

Where there's a will and a way, everything else is just details.

Information Today, **September 1999**

Funny, isn't it, how the month that houses Thanksgiving occurs before the month with all the presents? Maybe the sequence should teach us a moral lesson, that we should probe for things that deserve gratitude on our own and not count on thanks for all the gifts we give—at least not for another 11 months.

Information Today, **November 1997**

Remember the Gospel parable of the loaves and fishes .... The traditional interpretation of this incident, which I learned in religion class, was that Christ had multiplied the loaves and fishes through miraculous powers.

However, sometimes I think it might be nicer if the miracle occurred in another way. Maybe people who had just finished listening to a love-thy-neighbor message saw the baskets coming and pulled out their private food stashes they hadn't wanted to risk sharing with (or having snatched by) hungry bystanders. Maybe, as they reached in, they slipped their own food into the baskets. People changing for the better by heeding wise advice ... now that would be a real miracle.

Information Today, **June 1997**

Chapter 8

BQ ON BQ

Once a demure schoolgirl gently educated by nuns, Barbara somehow became a force of nature no searcher or database vendor can afford to ignore—a fact she is fully aware of, just as she is aware of all her little quirks and foibles. I can vouch for the fact that, though she herself nurtures her reputation for a sizable ego, she was not only pleased but surprised when I proposed this project. My guess is that, under the deadline pressure of two columns a month since 1986, she casually dropped pearls of wisdom and moved on to the next column without sensing the cumulative impact of her words. When presented with the rough draft of this manuscript, displaying the best of her writing over 15 years, her reaction was, if I may paraphrase, "Gee, did I say all that? Hey, not bad!"

The Early Days

Was there ever a time when I couldn't research? If I reach far enough back into the distant mists of prehistory, perhaps I can recall when I first learned to do research. I know it was before library school—that's where I learned to do it smart.

… I used to copy answers verbatim out of the *World Book Encyclopedia*. Some schoolmate once asked me whether I planned to rephrase my extracts—probably a fellow student who had reached the "P" volume. (Apparently, no one ever asked me to look up "plagiarism.") Even then, the incipient researcher within grew indignant that anyone could think that I would go so far as to threaten the purity of my research technique and imperil the absolute accuracy of my reporting by changing even a comma.

No matter how tired my pen hand grew, my meticulous transcribing never faltered. Looking back, either my teachers never read enough of my homework to suspect plagiarism or else the transcription process so contributed to my daily vocabulary that the work sounded as much like me as the *World Book*. Hmmmmm. Since the teachers were nuns and consecrated to diligence, let's suppose the latter, shall we?

Information Today, **March 1999**

My mother used to try to "guilt" me into productive action. I recall once, as a teenager, when she asked me a familiar question, "How can you just sit there and watch me work?" For the first time, I actually tried to answer what I had long considered a rhetorical question. I replied, "Actually, I kind of enjoy it. You're very good at what you do, you know. Remember when we went to your office last month and stopped to look through the holes in the fence next to that construction site. I figure that's why they put the holes there—because it's kind of fun to watch someone do what they know how to do well."

Information Today, **October 1997**

Sooner or later, someone's going to make you parallel park.

… There I was, a tender teenage driver wannabe with the inspector sitting by my side. With all my heart, I wanted to make the safest turn I would ever make in my life. In no way did I want to take any chances on the turn or the test. But I had no choice. There was no way to be absolutely sure no cars were coming. Oozing out too slowly would just have compounded the problem, but I didn't want to lunge out either ….

At that moment, I realized that life does not offer any guarantees, that sooner or later the only thing you can do is to go for it the best you can and trust in luck or ability to get you through, that the only alternative is spending the rest of your life as a passenger.

Searcher, **October 1994**

As a freshman in college, I journeyed to the local university campus for class assignments. How green was I? It was my first time in a real, full-size research library. In fact, I interpreted the closed stack policy as a tribute to my entrance into the world of the intellect. Imagine! The state appropriated funds just to make sure we scholars could continue our deep deliberations free from the burden of schlepping our own books.

And they called my number. They handed me a pile of books. On the top was a copy of John Locke's "Essay Concerning Human Understanding." The "s"s looked funny. They looked like "f"s without the crossbars. The book in my hand had been published 10 years after the original! The library had given me an 18th century printing. This great library trusted me as a member of the community of the mind and met my needs without regard to any risk to their possessions. Precious rare book or well-thumbed paperback, this great library taught me that the value of knowledge surpasses the value of its container.

Searcher, September 1994

My life as a professional searcher began back in the mid-'70s. The first online service our reference service used was AIMS-TWX—a pre-Medline search program from the National Library of Medicine. Grim? You have no idea. Every time we wanted to do a search, we had to call the computer department and book a TI700 300-baud (maximum) terminal. When they had one ready, we had to go up and drag the thing down. It was roughly equivalent in weight to a large fax machine, though it was long rather than squat. A year or so later, the library got a TI700 of its own. When we added the *New York Times* Information Service (NYTIS), equipment requirements launched us into the stratosphere of high-tech online communication speeds—1200-baud. Zowie!

Wilson Library Bulletin, February 1995

In the "I-can't-believe-I-survived-without-this-product" category, I can still recall crawling up an 8-foot ladder to reach back volumes of *Chemical Abstracts* in the dustiest, dirtiest, chilliest corner of a library sub-sub-basement. If they ever start making docudramas on the lives of information professionals (who knows how specialized cable channels can get?), I want the background theme from Disney's

The Rescuers for this sequence. That's the plaintive, lost-girl theme, not Aretha Franklin's "Rescue Me." Too much rocking and the ladder tips.

Information Today, **December 1996**

And dare we mention the revenue the Institute for Scientific Information would have lost over the years in making reparations to searchers who lost their sight trying to read the fine print in the paper version of *Science Citation Index*? Fortunately, online delivery stopped that potential fiscal hemorrhage before it started.

Information Today, **December 1996**

I shall never forget the look on an acquisitions librarian's face when she found me carefully editing off ISBN numbers before sending a printout to a client. I thought they made the search look tacky. Besides, the client wouldn't know what to do with them.

Document Delivery World, **March 1993**

The Women's Movement had a saying: "Scratch a woman, find a feminist."

Many, many years ago, I came to learn the truth of that saying and, in time, that the truth held beyond feminism. The moment of revelation still shines in my mind's eye.

A much younger (but still right and righteous) me sits in a restaurant arguing with an older woman about women's rights. We were polite, but we were both sincere and really going at it. She held very traditional views that marriage and children were the only course for every woman and that public policy should enforce that lifestyle completely. And she wouldn't budge.

Realizing that my arguments weren't getting anywhere, I finally paused, took a deep breath, and asked, "What about your daughter? You believe in marriage and children as the only right choice for yourself and women in general. But would you want your daughter to have no other options? Would you tell her never to get an advanced education or learn a profession? Would you want the Women's Movement to stop fighting for her right to that education or that good job? Are you that sure that whoever she marries will always take care of her—and her children, too?"

That got her! She quickly went silent and ceased arguing her position. You could see in her eyes the conflict between her general views and her values as a mother. She didn't want her daughter boxed into any irreversible disadvantage. And now she had to face the question of why she should espouse policies that would box in some other mother's daughter.

Information Today, November 1996

I Told Them, But Did They Listen To Me?

Someday soon, we may all sit down to a customized morning newspaper displayed on our electronic mail service or rolling off our fax machine. The newspaper would bear our name in the title and carry entertainment, financial, professional, and general news matching our specific interests. As the online industry designs a new generation of products to meet consumers' expectations—instead of trying to educate them about what to expect—information services and professionals could find a rapidly developing information market.

Wilson Library Bulletin, **June 1993**

When all is said and done, the phone companies can expand the market for newspaper product with little or no expense to the newspapers. Instead of finding themselves trapped with rising production costs and declining readerships and advertiser bases, newspapers would find themselves able to sell their product throughout the country with little additional marketing strain. Of course, it means that others can reach the newspapers' home markets, but technology has opened those markets anyway.

Information Today, **September 1992**

Chicken Little called the other day to tell me that the sky was falling. He was right. It did.

Excuse the note of bitterness. The friend/colleague who called had claimed to be a regular reader of my apparently all-too-humble writings. Yet, when he finally felt the full impact of the Internet and its Web personally, he immediately put in an emergency call to urge me to warn information professionals and the information industry about the enormous threat to their lives, their fortunes, and their sacred honor.

Oh, really? What a good idea. Now, why didn't I think of that? Harumph! What the heck do you think I've been doing for the last four or five years?! But this just goes to confirm what I've long suspected: Nobody is listening.

Information Today, **February 1997**

I told you, World, that online was the way to go. I told you, Information Industry, that someday this stuff would reach the masses. I told you, Techies, that someday people would buy computers just to make their modems work. I told you, Librarians, that people would expect information to pour out of a computer like water from a tap.

Information Today, **September 1997**

BQ and Computers: The Love-Hate Relationship

So how do you buy a machine in a disaster situation? Very quickly.

Searcher, **January 1995**

Before we continue this saga, I'd like to insert a public service announcement. You have read this far. You have placed your name on a routing list or purchased this periodical. You have made some commitment to the judgment of this editor. Stop reading this editorial! Stop and go straight to your computer. Where are your backup disks? Pick them up. What is the date marked clearly on the labels. Yes! It has been too long! Back up your computer now! And never, never, never let your back-up fall that far behind again.

Database Searcher, **January 1991**

Computer users experience hardware upgrades, like greatness, according to Mr. Shakespeare's flow chart. Some are born to upgrades, some achieve upgrades, and some have upgrades thrust upon them. So far, all my experiences of new equipment have fallen in the last category, but this year I will edge closer to the second.

Searcher, **January 1995**

I suppose some people are brave enough to move boards from inside one computer to inside another, but I consider such actions as rash, dangerous, and possibly obscene.

Searcher, **January 1995**

I like and trust written explanations. Yes. You have guessed it. Unlike any other computer user in history, I Do Read the Blankety-blank Manuals.

Searcher, **May 1995**

Already, a CD-ROM expert has advised me that if the disc won't run all by itself, if it has the audacity to expect me to read something before I use it ("Manuals! We don't need no stinkin' manuals!"), I should toss it in the trash. Really? Hey, that's a standard we dial-up junkies have been trying to impose on traditional search services for decades.

Wilson Library Bulletin, **March 1995**

[*Does she contradict herself? She is large, she contains multitudes.*]

I am in big, big trouble.

This new machine with its new software has started to come alive. It looks a lot like Frankenstein—and a Frankenstein with an Attitude. The attractions of this new life form seem relatively minor at the moment as I sit here with nervous eyes and a sickly placating grin on my face while The Creature lurches around my workplace smashing delicate equipment with unconscious abandon. The techno-lust that drove the original purchase seems just a ghost of a memory at the moment. I wonder what sort of penance priests give in the confessional for techno-lust. Right now, the admonition "Go thou and sin no more," would be a pleasure to obey.

Searcher, **May 1995**

You know, I don't want to be rude or anything, but have you guys reading this column ever considered getting a life of your own? I don't know how many calls or messages I've gotten over the last few months where people eagerly exclaim, "Oh, I've been reading your columns about your new computer. They're the first things I turn to. I just laugh and laugh."

Humph. Well, I'm glad my little difficulties have had some amusement value at least .… It's true what the grammarians say—tragedy is in the first person, comedy in the third person.

Searcher, **October 1995**

On Her Personal Foibles

The gentleman on the phone wanted to pump my brain for opinions on future developments in the online business information sector. (When you're registered at Guru Central, you get a lot of these kinds of calls—particularly if your entry carries the annotation "Will talk for compliments.")

Information Today, **October 1999**

"Never Being Wrong" has always been one of my most prized working skills as a columnist .... My faith is confirmed. The universe rights itself. I may not always be accurate, but I am never wrong.

Information Today, **September 1996**

Accusations of false modesty have never plagued my life. Occasionally, I wonder why. But then I guess the wondering explains why.

Searcher, **June 1996**

There's no getting around it. I'm no survivor. And I've got the test scores to prove it ....

Twice in my life, I have been lured into taking part in survival exercises. You know the kind—the ones that leave you and your team stranded in the burning desert or freezing in the arctic wilderness or, just as bad, the ones that posit post-nuclear bureaucratic crises. In both cases— whether environmentally or organizationally challenged—I flunked. When the exercises ended, there I sat—disgraced, unemployed road kill.

Searcher, **September 1999**

If there's one thing I hate, it's competition—unless, of course, it works to my advantage.

Searcher, **November/December 1995**

By nature, I lack discipline, but operate well on enthusiasm. Which means, if you can get me started, I may get engrossed and keep on going past the scheduled stopping point. The trick is self-starting the process.

Searcher, **May 1995**

Now, what do I plan to do with all this extra time? Good question. First, I'm going to read more. No, no. Not professional literature, well, not mainly. Books. All those tomes mounting up around the house bearing mute witness to my status as an Amazon-aholic. My reading will be eclectic, because lateral, leapfrog thinking that finds hidden linkages in apparently disparate material characterizes the process of growing wise.

Searcher, **February 2000**

In an orgy of Amazon-aholism, I purchased an 18-volume work of historical fiction set in the Napoleonic era aboard the ships of His Majesty's Britannic fleet .… Maybe I should have read one—just one!—book by the author before I purchased the entire set. Do ya think? Huh? Maybe? Argh! …

All the signs were favorable, but, nonetheless, so far the reading feels like rowing, if you get my nautical drift—too much strain for not enough gain. And there they sit—the remaining 17 volumes. But they will not wait in vain, because the only thing more psychotic than my urge to splurge on Amazon is my rigid compulsion to finish every book I start.

Information Today, **July/August 1999**

I am allergic to sesame seeds, Hawaiian music, and coercion. Each will quickly induce an automatic and uncontrollable revulsive reaction. My parents and I discovered this about sesame seeds as I sat with my head between my knees beside the discarded half of a hamburger next to their car, which by then sorely needed a wash. The sound of Hawaiian music—particularly steel guitars—actually provokes in me a grimace that seems to screw my entire face in a 360-degree turn.

But coercion …. Well, coercion causes a much more severe reaction, a prolonged and utterly committed resistance. I hate being boxed. I hate seeing or hearing about anyone being boxed. I hate boxing other people in, even when it's to my advantage. There's something about that trapped animal image, something about callous triumph vs. panicked vulnerability. I just can't stand it. And my compulsive reaction is to stop it at almost any price, or at the very least to make the coercer pay—somehow, sometime, somewhere. You can lead me, cajole me, or just ask me, and I'll most likely follow your path. But honey, don't push. Never push.

Information Today, **June 1996**

Many, many moons ago, pinned down by a lynch mob of vendor representatives all shouting "Troublemaker!!

Troublemaker!," I squealed out my standard excuse, "I don't look for trouble. Trouble looks for me!" But what still amazes me is how diligently it finds me.

Searcher, **May 2000**

On Her Professional Accomplishments

My own *Searcher* is probably considered the most aggressive of the online trade press sources. The magazine and I, as its editor, were once introduced at an information industry trade association meeting as the "pit bull of the online trade press."

Wilson Library Bulletin, **March 1993**

See, information industry executives, Trouble doesn't only make me snarly. It also makes me complimentary. The secret is being on the Right Side of Trouble.

Searcher, **February 1997**

Sometimes, when I've been away from searching for a while, I physically want to touch the keyboard. I hunger for a search. My fingers start to twitch. Then, when I sit down to do a search and really get rolling, there is a sense of being a pianist, of somebody whose fingers twiddle over the keys and magically, information is summoned ....

The best time is when you feel really clever. When clients give you an impossible task, even one they don't think you can answer, and you pull it off with a smirk … that's sublime.

"Barbara Quint: Grasshopper Searcher."
In *Secrets of the Super Searchers*. 1993

Many, many years ago, I got my first speaking engagement with the Information Industry Association (IIA). It was only a regional meeting, but, frankly, I was thrilled. Golly! Gee! Speaking in front of the folks who actually made the databases I had used for so many years! Representing users everywhere, the Silent Majority whose Voice I could become, a Voice that would peal forth for all the Muted and Oppressed. Neat-o!

Searcher, **February 1997**

I learned that I like to ad-lib and that others don't. Spontaneous speakers give a touch of random energy to any program that keeps participants alert. And then there's the "comic relief" element. False modesty shall not deter me from telling you that I got a spontaneous round of applause at the close of the meeting, but I am prouder that I also got heckled and the heckler had a following.

Searcher, **February 1997**

Baby, I was searching full text before you were a gleam in a rug rat's eye. I AM Natural Language Processing. Your machines are just learning to catch up.

Searcher, **May 1999**

What measuring stick could I use to measure my career? … A-ha! I've got it. Let's count my career accomplishments in terms of gripes. With this column, I celebrate my 10,000th complaint and hereby award a Virtual Medal to the Virtuous Me, the Loyal Order of the Eternal Nag.

Searcher, **April 1996**

I am many things—an American, a Catholic, a feminist, a movie buff, a Californian, etc. I even belong to several occupational categories—writer, consultant, small business owner, and probably some more titles whose names and deadlines have escaped me.

But when ultimate truths are spoken, when the midnight of the soul is reached by any self-addressed, pre-stamped survey form's request for my occupation—then I know I am a Librarian.

Database Searcher, **September 1990**

Philosophy of Life

What remains is Quint's First Law of Politics—"Never attribute to conspiracy what can be fully explained by stupidity." (I used to dabble in intelligence literature in a former job.)

Information Today, **June 1995**

Before 1999 ended, I'd decided to make a few larger-than-life New Year's resolutions for the Big 2K. By the time you start reading this editorial, I'll have probably already breached most of those resolutions, added enough mitigating clauses to others to turn them into paper tigers, and maybe even abandoned some altogether. But what the heck? As the wise G. K. Chesterton once observed, "A thing worth doing is worth doing badly."

Searcher, **February 2000**

Even if we start in the right direction, trip and fall, pick ourselves up, start off again, wander off course, fall asleep, and get arrested for vagrancy, at least we'll have tried to seek a better path, to break out of the one-foot-after-another rut, to take a new lead. As another wiseacre once said, "Life is like the Iditarod race. If you're not the lead dog, the view never changes."

Searcher, **February 2000**

The grand goal of my resolutions, for example, is Wisdom. All in all, I would like to grow wiser in the years ahead. Wealth and immortality also have their attractions, but realistically, my professional skills and personal character would seem to make Wisdom a more pragmatic goal.

Searcher, **February 2000**

Survival just isn't enough. When [*William Faulkner*] gave his Nobel Prize acceptance speech, he predicted that mankind would not merely endure, it would prevail. That's the way I look at life, don't you? Why just endure when you could prevail?

Searcher, **September 1999**

Chapter 9

BQ'S FANS SPEAK OUT

Let me start with my own favorite bq story: At the SCOUG meeting at Internet Librarian 2000, Carole Leita, who created Librarians' Index to the Internet (http://lii.org), asked why so few California libraries used it on their own home pages. Another librarian explained that the Librarians' Index was just too big, and kind of intimidating for their users, but if they could get a smaller version of it, with only a few top resources for each category, her library would be interested.

Barbara pointed to the President of the Association of Independent Information Professionals and told Carole Leita, "That's the woman you want to talk to. AIIP is full of the kind of people who can do the slicing and dicing for you, right?" The AIIP President agreed on the spot. (Not that she had much choice.)

Problem stated, problem explained, solution delivered, in five minutes flat. When I congratulated Barbara afterward on a masterful performance, she was surprised I was making a big deal out of it—for her, it was just one more day in the life.

It's hard to believe that eight years of *Searcher* have been published since that fateful day when Barbara called me to discuss how we might collaborate on a new periodical. It seemed that Mecklermedia, the publisher of Barbara's

Database Searcher, was getting out of the library and information professional field, and Barbara was left high and dry without an outlet for her editorial product. "Why don't we do a new and better magazine but simply call it *Searcher*?" she asked.

I guess I acted as a prudent businessperson should react. I wrote a business plan, had numerous meetings with my staff, and, after sufficiently agonizing over every detail, finally agreed to go forward. In retrospect, however, I needn't have worried. I should've just handed Barbara the keys to the convertible and told her to have a good time at the party. She has never disappointed her publisher or her readers and shows no signs of running out of ideas or creative juices.

I have to admit to a few anxious moments when Barbara "called it like she saw it" and spoke her mind about one product or another that she didn't feel lived up to its billing. Barbara is rarely shy about such things, and, yes, we've had some phone calls. But she's always fair and open minded, and even her critics respect her integrity and professionalism.

When our industry starts handing out its own "lifetime achievement" awards, Barbara should be at the head of the line. In the meantime, Barbara, let me just say congratulations on a job very well done!

Tom Hogan, President, Information Today, Inc.,
in an e-mail message, December 28, 2000.

What Clapton is to the guitar, what Jordan is to the court, Barbara Quint is to online searching—the pro the other pros admire. She is well known as a researcher, consultant, author, speaker, and editor. Whichever hat she is wearing, she is always the Ralph Nader of the online world, an articulate and relentless advocate for the online consumer. (The Nader comparison is not perfect; Ralph is quite proper and a little grim, but Barbara's take-no-prisoners style and whiplash sense of humor guarantee standing-room-only crowds wherever she speaks.)

Mick O'Leary. *Link-Up*, **May-June 1993**

Who is Barbara, what is she, that all database searchers from West to East, South to North, belong to her extensive fan club? Ask anyone, she's simply a fantastically knowledgeable and dedicated online expert.

... I've often invited her to participate in my conference programs and she's never shy about her ability to draw crowds. That's how I got hooked, as others do, on her rapid and razor-sharp wit at the podium. You are either captivated by Barbara's brand of public speaking or you're not. But I can't think of one single online searcher who wouldn't bet the company's database terminal on her.

Nancy Melin Nelson, *Information Today*, **September 1991**

From a writer's viewpoint, a skilled editor is more than someone who doesn't mince your words. A truly gifted editor can persuade you to take on assignments that you're reluctant, out of fear of potential humiliation and professional ruin, to accept.

bq is a great editor.

Reva Basch. *Searcher*, **January 2000**

What sticks in my mind about bq isn't a particular bon mot or deep, insightful comment on the online industry, but the peculiar texture of our personal relationship over the years, which I'd describe as one of mutual respect shot through with sarcasm. Two examples: After I made the mistake of telling her how much a particular computer magazine paid—relative to what *Searcher* paid its writers—she started referring to me—incessantly and publicly—as "$2-a-word-Reva."

At one summer's SCOUG retreat, I went hiking with two colleagues during a break, and we encountered a rattlesnake on the trail. The story got around, and when we reconvened for business later that day, bq couldn't resist making a comment that involved me, the rattlesnake, and the phrase "professional courtesy." She's inimitable—thank goodness.

Reva Basch, in an e-mail message, November 27, 2000.

I have known Barbara well over 20 years, almost since graduating library school at UCLA. Since I have been in the vendor side for about half of those years, sometimes it has been a plus to know her (she was one of my references when I applied to Dialog) and sometimes it has been difficult (especially when she goes after a company I work for and people think I am the unnamed source—which I am not). But she is a remarkable woman and an extraordinary asset to our industry, and I am proud to know her.

At a SCOUG Steering Committee meeting some years ago, about 10 of us were crowded around the table, scarfing down mediocre pizza and trying to get the meeting on track (they never stay on track, even with an agenda). We were talking about an upcoming workshop, whose overall coordinator, Dudee Chiang, had been somewhat reluctant to take charge because it was well known that SCOUG members have great ideas, but it's sometimes a challenge to get them to meet their commitments on calling folks, making arrangements with hotels, and all the other tasks.

We all agreed that we needed to respond to the coordinator's pleas. At the exact same moment, Barbara and I both shouted out, "So remember ... When Dudee calls, answer!"

We all started roaring with laughter, even Dudee.

Barbara has a million of these one-liners and inside jokes she can make effortlessly. I have always been proud that for one moment in time, Barbara and I were on the exact same wavelength.

Patti Brown Finie, of the Gale Group,
in an e-mail message, September 29, 2000.

In the beginning was the laugh. I'd heard the name and, from time to time, I would buy a lone, crumpled copy of *Searcher* from an Oakland newsstand, but before I met Barbara Quint, there was the laugh, rumbling from a back corner of the room. Steve Coffman had invited me to speak at SCOUG's Annual Spring Workshop and I had no idea what kind of people were in the room or that everything was about to change. Librarians, he'd said, information people of all stripes. "Come," he said, "It'll be fun." So there I was in a hotel ballroom, lights out, microphone on, singing my Powerpoint song when I first became aware of the laugh.

... The laugh was unusual. Intriguing. It sounded both practiced and delighted. It established a kind of harmony with my rhythm and urged me to be more outrageous. Yes, lots of others were laughing (she said modestly) but I could tell that this laugh mattered and was leading the pack.

While introductions were made all around, it wasn't until my first SCOUG summer retreat a few months later that I identified Barbara as the owner of the laugh. Though it's possible that because she'd heard my talk, she'd gotten my number, I have since come to see that Barbara Quint was born knowing this number and quite a few others. I've watched her, in the years since, engage with old friends and new and she treats them all exactly alike. First, there is the grin and the "Hey you!" (which is bq shorthand for "Of course I know your name, let's not waste time on conventional stuff like that"), then a pause (operatic, yet sincere) while her eyes travel over your face. "How are you?" she says, "Are you okay? Is there anything I can do for you?" And she means it.

But you had better move fast during that pause because this is the last moment you'll be standing on firm ground. Barbara is like the genie in the bottle: she grants wishes, she lays out options, she dispenses phone numbers, she offers to summon up the demons of hell if someone hasn't been treating you in the way you deserve. You begin to understand that the genie can't, won't, go back in the bottle. Events will be set in motion from that point forward and it's no good at all reverting to your sensible self and asking for moderation.

Let's say, however, that you are just fine and you need nothing, really Barbara, nothing at all. Barbara will begin the conversation proper by throwing out a zinger, her lead sentence, the hook. Is it some clever thing by Chesterton she's just been reading? (Question: Am I the only one who gets a lot of Chesterton? Please call me if there are other possibilities.) Maybe it's an idiot statement she just picked up for the newswire, a Supreme Court decision, something Admiral Nelson once said during the Punic Wars? (Yes, you can drift a bit here.)

Then you are well and truly off and running. Barbara is the only Socratic angel I know. She'll take something you said that was perfectly obvious and show you how you could look at it upside down and declare total victory. She'll take something you said that was perfectly true and show you that you couldn't possibly have meant it that way.

Is this just a little bit alarming? You bet. But stick it out and you'll see that whatever goes into Barbara's blender comes out as a tasty treat which she will pour into an icy glass, garnish with mint, twist it once on the tray, and present with a flourish. The last time I saw Barbara, she told me that when she meets a political person, someone who loves to "mix it up," she can't help urging them to use this power for good. "You get to have," she said with a chuckle, "the very same fun messing with other people's lives that you can have with an evil agenda. And you get all that good karma too."

The minute I walked into that first SCOUG event, Barbara began messing with me and I hope it never ends. As a public librarian, a (former) civil servant, someone who has been to countless meetings devoted to "we considered doing that once in 1976 and it didn't work," I am not a big believer in organizations. SCOUG is my one exception. When the C. G. Jung Institute of Northern California was first established, they wrote to Jung to ask for his blessing. His response was, "If you must have an institute, make it as disorganized as possible." Not only could Jung have joined SCOUG simply by attending a meeting and getting on the mailing list, he'd have volunteered for something, I just know it.

I can now hear Barbara in her editorial guise asking me to wrap it up, add two, maybe three more clever statements, take it back to the laugh and tie it all together. You'd never expect a woman like this to be the sort of patient (yet relentless in pursuit) editor that she is.

Here's the image I have, at least when she's working with me: I feel like a child actor in the hands of John Huston. (Has anyone mentioned how much Barbara loves film?) Though he is capable of terror when called for, Huston doesn't want to tamper with my spontaneity and he's cast me for my awkward charm. So he approaches me quietly and without stooping. He is taller than me, that is clear, so why pretend to be child-sized? This puts me at ease—at last, an adult who admits to being an adult! He asks me first what I want to do with this scene. He thinks about it without saying a word. Yes, he says, that would be very, very good.

And while Barbara will call and tell me that Huston never did this or that, and that a better story about child actors is the time that so and so did this or that, and that she'll never forget how in the Hope/Crosby on-the-road pictures, the director once said (and now this is a run-on sentence), I will be rewarded, as I always am, by the laugh that leads the pack. You can learn a lot from a laugh like that.

Mary-Ellen Mort, Project Director, JobStar California, in an e-mail message, November 15, 2000.

INDEX

Y

ABOUT THE EDITOR

Marylaine Block, "writer, internet trainer, and librarian without walls," was a librarian at St. Ambrose University for 22 years, where she constructed a Web site for her campus known as "Best Information on the Net." As one of the earliest librarian indexes to the Net, it garnered her a reputation as a "guru" (moral: get there first), but it also indirectly led to her being offered the opportunity to write a weekly online column, "My Word's Worth," for a British online magazine. This column led to an offer to write another weekly column, "Observing Us," which ran for two and a half years at Fox News online. Since then, she has published articles about the Internet in *Searcher*, *Library Journal*, *American Libraries*, *Yahoo! Internet Life*, and other magazines. She quit her day job to work full time as a writer, speaker, and internet trainer, but she has never stopped being a librarian at heart. She writes two weekly e-zines to serve the library community: *Neat New Stuff I Found This Week*, which reviews reference-quality internet sites, and *ExLibris*, where she talks about such issues as censorship, information, searching, and library Web site design. Her work can be viewed at http://marylaine.com.

More Great Books
from Information Today, Inc.

International Business Information on the Web
Searcher Magazine's Guide to Sites and Strategies for Global Business Research

By Sheri R. Lanza • Edited by Barbara Quint

This is the first ready-reference for effective worldwide business research. Helps readers identify overseas buyers, find foreign suppliers, investigate potential partners and competitors, uncover international market research and industry analysis, and much more. Supported by a Web site.

ISBN 0-910965-46-3 • $29.95

The Invisible Web
Uncovering Information Sources Search Engines Can't See

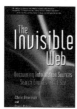

By Chris Sherman and Gary Price

Most of the authoritative information accessible over the Internet is invisible to search engines. This information resides on the "Invisible Web," which is largely comprised of content-rich databases from universities, libraries, associations, businesses, and government agencies. This guide is supported by a dedicated Web site.

ISBN 0-910965-51-X • $29.95

The Extreme Searcher's Guide to Web Search Engines
A Handbook for the Serious Searcher, 2nd Edition

By Randolph Hock • Foreword by Reva Basch

In this revised and expanded version of his award-winning book, the "extreme searcher," Ran Hock, digs even deeper, covering all the most popular Web search tools, plus a half-dozen of the newest and most exciting search engines to come down the pike. A practical, user-friendly guide supported by a regularly updated Web site.

ISBN 0-910965-47-1 • $24.95

Great Scouts!
CyberGuides for Subject Searching on the Web

By Nora Paul and Margot Williams
Edited by Paula Hane

Here is a cure for information overload. Authors Paul and Williams direct readers to the very best subject-specific, Web-based information resources. Thirty chapters cover the premier Internet sources of information on business, education, arts and entertainment, science and technology, health and medicine, politics and government, law, and much more. Expert advice and evaluations of content, value, currency, stability, and usability.

ISBN 0-910965-27-7 • $24.95

Electronic Democracy
Using the Internet to Transform American Politics, 2nd Edition

By Graeme Browning
Foreword by Adam Clayton Powell III

In this new edition of *Electronic Democracy*, award-winning journalist and author Graeme Browning details the colorful history of politics and the Net, describes the key Web-based sources of political information, offers practical techniques for influencing legislation online, and provides a fascinating, realistic vision of the future.

ISBN 0-910965-41-2 • $19.95

net.people
The Personalities and Passions Behind the Web Sites

By Eric C. Steinert and Thomas E. Bleier

In *net.people*, 36 entrepreneurs and visionaries share their personal stories and hard-won secrets of Webmastering. You'll learn how each of them launched a home page, increased site traffic, geared up for e-commerce, found financing, dealt with failure and success, built new relationships—and discovered that a Web site had changed their life forever.

ISBN 0-910965-37-4 • $19.95

Super Searchers Cover the World
The Online Secrets of International Business Researchers

By Mary Ellen Bates • Edited by Reva Basch

Through interviews with 15 leading searchers, Mary Ellen Bates explores the challenges of reaching outside a researcher's geographic area to do effective international business research. Librarians and researchers from government organizations, multinational companies, universities, and small businesses discuss such issues as non-native language sources, cultural biases, and the reliability of information.

ISBN 0-910965-54-4 • $24.95

Super Searchers Go to the Source
The Interviewing & Hands-On Information Strategies of Top Primary Researchers—Online, on the Phone, & in Person

By Risa Sacks • Edited by Reva Basch

For the most current, in-depth information on any subject, nothing beats going directly to the source—to the experts. This is "Primary Research," and it's the focus of the seventh title in the Super Searchers series. From the boardrooms of America's top corporations, to the halls of academia, to the pressroom of *The New York Times*, Risa Sacks interviews 12 of the best primary researchers in the business.

ISBN 0-910965-53-6 • $24.95

Super Searchers on Mergers & Acquisitions
The Online Research Secrets of Top Corporate Researchers and M&A Pros

By Jan Davis Tudor • Edited by Reva Basch

Here is a unique resource for business owners, brokers, appraisers, entrepreneurs, and investors who use the Internet and online services to research Mergers & Acquisitions (M&A) opportunities. Jan Davis Tudor interviews 13 top M&A researchers, who share their secrets for finding, evaluating, and delivering critical deal-making data on companies and industries.

ISBN 0-910965-48-X • $24.95

Super Searchers in the News
The Online Secrets of Journalists & News Researchers

Paula J. Hane • Edited by Reva Basch

Professional news researchers work under intense deadline pressure to meet the insatiable, ever-changing research needs of reporters, editors, and journalists. Here, for the first time, 10 news researchers reveal their strategies for using the Internet and online services to get the scoop, check the facts, and nail the story.

ISBN 0-910965-45-5 • $24.95

Super Searchers on Health & Medicine
The Online Secrets of Top Health & Medical Researchers

Susan M. Detwiler • Edited by Reva Basch

Skilled medical researchers rank among the best online searchers in the world. In this book, medical librarians, clinical researchers, health information specialists, and physicians explain how they combine traditional sources with the best of the Net to deliver just what the doctor ordered. These Super Searchers guide you to the best sites, sources, and techniques.

ISBN 0-910965-44-7 • $24.95

Super Searchers on Wall Street
Top Investment Professionals Share Their Online Research Secrets

By Amelia Kassel • Edited by Reva Basch

Amelia Kassel reveals the online secrets of 10 leading financial industry research experts. You'll learn how information professionals find and analyze market and industry data, as well as how online information is used by brokerages, stock exchanges, investment banks, and individual investors to make critical investment decisions.

ISBN 0-910965-42-0 • $24.95

The OPL Sourcebook
A Guide for Solo and Small Libraries

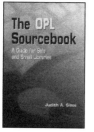

By Judith A. Siess

Judith A. Siess, editor of the monthly newsletter, *The One-Person Library*, has created the definitive handbook and directory for small and one-person libraries (OPLs). Taking an international approach to reflect the growing number of OPLs worldwide, this new book covers organizational culture, customer service, time management and planning, budgeting, accounting, technology, collection development, education, downsizing, outsourcing, and many other key management issues. Includes a comprehensive directory.

ISBN 1-57387-111-7 • $39.50

The Modem Reference
The Complete Guide to PC Communications, 4th Edition

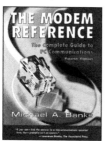

By Michael A. Banks

This popular handbook explains the concepts behind computer data, data encoding, and transmission, providing practical advice for PC users who want to get the most from their online operations. In his uniquely readable style, author and techno-guru Michael A. Banks (*The Internet Unplugged*) takes readers on a tour of PC data communications technology, explaining how modems, fax machines, computer networks, and the Internet work and demystifying the terminology, hardware, and software.

ISBN 0-910965-36-6 • $29.95